Medieval Times & the Knight in Shining Armor

Biography of an Ancient

By Nesenty

Copyright © 2011 by Nesenty

ISBN: 1460938194
EAN-13: 978-1460938195

All rights reserved. No part of this book may be reproduced or transmitted in any form or by any means, electronic or mechanical, including photocopying, recording, or by any information storage and retrieval system, without permission in writing from the copyright owner.

This book was printed in the United States of America.

Introduction

After having my body placed into a coma like state, I concentrated on forcing my mind from my body. They would wait until the energy signatures remained at a low level before placing my body into stasis, to ensure that I was out of it and was capable of keeping the spirit separated from the physical form. It took me a week to convince myself that I needed not my body as I was accustomed to, once that was settled, I focused on Earth. As everything went black for a moment, it was as if I opened my eyes from closing them, I saw green land around me, buildings in the distance. As I got closer, I took note of the fact that they were simple structures, wooden sides and thatched roofs. Watching the people as they moved around, they wore different clothing than the other two times I had been here. People moved about, doing labors and talking to each other, children ran and played.

I needed to find a body that was dying, I needed to get permission from the person occupying it. I spent the next three days listening to people talk, trying to keep my spirit from returning home, remembering which ones I had overheard. It seemed no one was dying in this village right now, I was about ready to leave here when I overheard someone asking "how is she?"

Turning I saw an older woman talking to a young boy, in his later childhood years, almost fully grown. He had blonde hair, a small build, blue eyes. I looked him over from head to toe, waiting for him to answer the older woman who had gray hair, ice blue eyes and a thin build as well.

"She does not improve." He choked out.

"The fever has set in and taken hold?" The woman asked, looking sad.

"Priest comes to give her last rights, he fears she will not last more than a few days."

"She will be with God." The woman placed her hand on the boys shoulder, squeezing gently.

'I must follow this boy, the she that they speak of is dying. I may have found a body here after all.' I thought to myself.

"She has not eaten a thing for a week, nor drank for a day. She barely..." he was beginning to cry, "she does not wake often."

"The fever does this, it takes those we love from us. But we can take comfort in the fact that there will be angels to take her to God. She has been good, he will welcome her." The woman tried to console the boy.

"I must get this back to mother, she asked that I pick it up..." he swallowed hard. "Father will be home with the priest soon."

"Give your mother and father my love." The woman nodded, walking away from the boy.

He was holding a basket of cloth, they looked like rags inside of it, just scraps of fabric. He stiffened his back, straightening and forcing the tears to stop before they ran down his face anymore. As he walked off I followed behind him, watching as he carried the basket in his arms. Coming to the end of the street, he turned towards a little shack. Not much more than sticks it holding it upright, dried grass lay on a bottom layer for the roof, covered by greener, fresher grass tied to the top. Following him inside there was a woman sitting at a table, she looked tired, worn. Long blonde hair braided at her neck that fell down her back. The boy set the basket down and immediately went to stand next to her, resting his hand on her shoulder. They stood there, not saying a word to one another.

Looking around the building, there was not much to it. I noticed a door cracked towards the back of the building, moving towards it I sensed the change in energy. Instead of sadness, I now felt sickness, I felt the energy become thicker the closer I got to the door. Moving through it I went into the room, the energy was so thick it almost choked me out. There was a young girl laying on the bed, two blankets thrown over her, a cloth sitting on her head, her eyes were closed. She was dying and there was nothing the people here could do to help. Her spirit was stuck inside of her body for now, she hung on for what little time she had left. Moving towards her, I sat on the edge of the bed, next to her legs, her arms were folded over her stomach.

Reaching for her, I laid my hand on top of hers, connecting to who she was inside, not just the physical form on the outside. I sensed what was wrong with her, it was an infection, set in from a cut she had received earlier in her life and spread through her blood stream. She grew ill, then the fever had started, making her too weak to defend against outside bacteria. If I had been in my physical form, I could have healed her, at least tried. There was nothing I could do for her in the form that I was in. I could only try to comfort her until she died, hopefully she could connect to me. I needed permission before I could use another beings body. Honestly, I did not need permission, but that was the difference between some and others, it was the right thing to do.

As the sun began to set it began to grow dark in the

building, I heard the voices outside of the room.

"Is she?" A man's voice asked.

"No father, she is sleeping still." The boy answered.

"The priest has come to give her last rights." The man continued, "this is Father Mathew."

"Hello Father." The woman said, "Catherine is just in the other room."

"How... has she been peaceful?" Another man's voice said.

"Yes. She sleeps most of the time, the worst passed a few days ago. She no longer thrashes in pain." The woman answered.

"The time is near then my children, take me to her so that she may be ushered into our Father's waiting arms."

I heard the door behind me open, turning my head I saw the woman come in, followed by a man holding her hand, another man in a black dress carrying a book, and the boy behind him. The man in the dress stepped close to the bed, he wore something around his neck that hung down, a small cap on the top of his head, another dress underneath the black one that was white, the book in his hand and a belt around his middle that held a pouch to it. He looked at the girl in the bed, *Catherine*.

Removing a small glass bottle from his pouch, he set it on the small table beside the bed. Opening the book he carried he began to read from it, "God is our refuge and strength, a very presence to help in trouble. Therefore will not we fear, though the earth be removed, and though the mountains be carried into the midst of the sea, though the waters thereof roar and be troubled, though the mountains shake with the swelling thereof. There is a river, the streams whereof shall make glad the city of God, the holy place of the tabernacles of the most High. God is in the midst of her, she shall not be moved, God shall help her, and that right early. The heathen raged, the kingdoms were moved, he uttered his voice, the earth melted. The Lord of hosts is with us, the God of Jacob our refuge. Come, behold the worlds of the Lord, what desolation's he hath made in the earth. He maketh wars to cease unto the end of the earth, he breaketh the bow, and cutteth the spear in sunder, he burned the chariot in fire. Be still, and know that I am God, I will be exalted among the heathen, I will be exalted in the earth. The Lord of hosts is with us, the God of Jacob is our refuge." Stopping, he closed his book and set it down, picking up the small bottle he had set down, he removed the cork from the top, placing two fingers over the top and turning it sideways he wet his fingers. Placing his fingers on Catherine's forehead, he moved them downwards and lifted them slightly, moving his fingers across her forehead this time. "Per istam sanctam unctionem, indulgeat tibi Dominus quidquid deliquisti, Amen." Setting the bottle down he re-corked it and turned back to her, "Go with God my child, may the Lord and Savior send messengers to escort you into his kingdom of Heaven." He waved his hand over her body, drawing down from her head to her chest, and then crossing over her chest again.

The woman was hugging the man behind him crying, the boy stood there, eyes closed, listening, his hands clasped in front of him. I didn't know what was going on, nor what they were doing or what the man in the dress had done to her.

As the man picked up his book, replacing his bottle into the pouch on his belt he turned around to the woman and man, their son, "Let us pray." Leading them from the room they shut the door slightly behind them.

Turning my focus back on the girl, I sat there, holding her hand and staying with her while she slept. I sat there through the night, as the moon rose in the sky and the man in the dress was in the other room with the parents and brother, reciting who knows what, probably from that book of his. He never stopped talking.

As the sun began to peek in the sky, giving warmth to the Earth once again, Catherine began to stir, opening her eyes slightly she looked right at me. I smiled at her, watching as she tried to smile back at me. Leaning forward I rested my hand on her head, whispering into her mind, "t'will only ease your pains, do not be afraid. Death does not end your life." She nodded at me, having heard me, watching me closely. Whispering into her mind again I explained, "I am in need of a body... I cannot take one without permission, and the vessel must be empty. I am here only to teach, not to harm anyone. When you go to the next life, may I use yours?"

She watched me a while longer, forcing her eyes open further, her energy tensed in her hand under mine, as if she was trying to squeeze my hand. She began moving her lips around, as if she was trying to wet them. "Y... yes..." she finally breathed out, nodding her head slightly.

"I will remain here with you until you are ready to go. I will not leave your side." I smiled at her. She was close if she could see me, her spirit was beginning to separate from the physical form, it was the only way that she could see me. The people of this planet did not have the correct vibrations to see through the veil of this life and the next, it required them to be on the edge of the between.

I sat there through the day as the mother and father came in, saying goodbye to her while she slept. As the brother came in, kneeling beside her and weeping until his shoulders shook. The man in the dress had left after talking all night long. Everyone was waiting, waiting for her to die as if there was nothing else to do. There was not anything else they could do, they could not heal her, they could not soothe her pain, all they could do is sit by her but they seemed fearful of that. Almost as if she would cause them to become ill as well.

As the sun began to set, I watched her sleep, peace falling over her as her pain subsided, her body was beginning to shut down. One organ at a time. She would not make it through the night.

Opening her eyes, she looked at me again. She could not speak, but she could still think. I replaced my hand on her head, listening to the whispered thoughts of her mind. "What will it be like?"

"I do not know." I thought back, shaking my head. I had never died before, not in the sense that she was, I always returned to my body, my home. Where she was going was the next life, I did not know what that would bring for her, I could not answer her with the knowledge she wanted, but I could tell her of what I did know. "It is said, there is no pain there. No loss. It is summer all the time with green grasses and trees growing, blue waters and warmth all the time. Always light."

"Tis coming is it?" She wanted to know if she was getting close.

"Yes." I nodded. "Your physical body is shutting down. You will begin to loose feeling in it, and feel a weight on you as if you are held down before your spirit departs the physical form." It was much like astral travel, the physical body hung on until you forced it loose. The first few times were always the hardest.

"I am ready." She thought to me.

"I know." The energy around her was changing, it felt thinner and more relaxed, it felt peaceful.

"You may use the body." She tried to smile as she thought it.

"Thank you." I smiled at her as she shut her eyes. Letting her mind and the body rest.

Putting my hand back on hers along with the other one, I sat there with her as her breathing slowed. The rise and fall of her chest slowed down until it barely rose at all. As I sensed her energy leaving the physical form I turned towards the direction she had moved in. Standing there next to the bed, she saw her body take it's last few breaths as it completely shut down. She looked at me and smiled. I nodded my head and watched as her spirit began to disappear, it faded into the room and went on to the next life.

Standing, I watched the body for a second, hopefully they would not burn it. I could force it through the Earth if they buried it, but if they burnt it, it would be a wasted trip, I would wake in my own body back home. Moving over I laid on top of her body, my back to her chest and focused my energy on melting into it. Feeling as my spirit moved into the physical form she had left, I began to feel that heavy feeling you get when you leave your body, a weight setting in over my chest and hers. Melting it into the physical form. Once inside, I could sense the changes beginning to take place. Areas of the body and the organs beginning to reactivate, start up again. I could not open it's eyes or see around me, nor could I hear around, but I could feel the body as it came to life again, slowly. First the organs would revive themselves, and then the blood would begin to move and rewrite some of it's genetics. It would be a day or so before I would be able to move the body or use it, but while I was waiting, the body would in a sense, wake up from it's sleep. I hoped they would not burn it again, one last time, and let my mind rest, sleeping inside of the body until both could wake together.

Chapter One

Waking up in the body I had taken, I could feel their heartbeat for the first time again. She had died not 2 days ago, what had possessed her family to leave her in the woods, I don't know. Maybe it was because she had been sick those last few months, maybe it was their traditions, I am not sure. She was young though, 19 years at the most, the body would last a while.

Getting up from the ground, I looked around, the trees were different than the first time I had been here, they no longer spoke. The grass and bush no longer danced with you, the animals I could hear became silent when you looked at them. I had come back, hoping to find the world as I had left it before all those years ago, instead I found a world that was dead. I had watched the people in the village for a time, watched and sat with this girl as she passed away, she had even seen me in those last moments, given me her permission.

'How far away from the town am I?' I asked myself as I caught the scent of water on the breeze that was blowing.

Knowing I should wash the body before going near anyone, I picked up the cloth I had been covered in up off the ground and made my way towards the water. On my way there I thought over what I had been told before I left, the request I had made to have my body put into stasis again, I wanted to return to Earth. *'You'll be on you own. We will not interact with them again at this point, we won't transfer your consciousness so you'll have to find an empty vessel to assume control of.*' My King had meant it when he said it, I was completely on my own from the moment I was placed into stasis.

Reaching the rivers edge, I thought nothing of the customs that were in place in this time, shucking the clothes from the body, I waded into the chilly water. Scrubbing the hair that fell over my shoulders and the body down with damp moss and sand. Reaching out I grabbed the clothes and began to wash them, again using the sand and moss to clean them. I could sense someone's presence, looking up I saw an animal drinking from the river. Sand colored fur, glistening white antlers, a black snout, and eyes that seemed to fear my presence.

'*It's okay.*' I thought to it, moving slowly. '*I am a friend. I will not harm you.*' Reaching my hand out slowly, to let it smell me. Just when I thought it would trust me, it spooked, turned and sprinted into the trees.

Something had happened between the times I had been here, the life here had grown to fear each other. It saddened me to realize the world had gone so wrong, everything seemed to *want* to interact, but the fear ingrained in them was so strong it prevented it. Wading back out of the water the sun was warm, but the breeze held a chill to it, and against the wet skin it was almost freezing. Instead of waiting for the cloth of the dress to dry, I closed my eyes and concentrated on the heat of my hands, warming the cloth, drying it with my heat.

Once it was dry, I held it, bending slightly and stepping into it, pulling it up over my hips and shoulders. Tying it at the back as far up as I could reach. What had possessed these people to tie clothing in the back, instead of on the side or in the front was beyond me. They had become backwards in all that they did.

Walking back into the tree's I gathered dry wood from the ground as I went. The ground was covered in leaves and soft grass, but every so often there would be a thorn that would stick into one of my feet. They had left this body, with little clothing, a cloth thrown over it, shoeless. It was not as if I had not gone shoeless most of my time, either back home or here, honestly there were very few times that I ever wore anything on my feet, but the thorns protruding into the skin did present a problem. When I had to stop every ten or so paces to pull the thorn from the bottom of a foot. It gave me a chance to look around though, so it could have been a good thing, if your into looking at the positive of situations. The birds and animals in the woods watched me, every step I took. They sensed something different, but the fear in them still made them uneasy.

I made my way to the other side of the forest, where the treeline broke into a field. Looking out the grass was so tall, it was as if I was watching the waves of an ocean once again. I remembered my time on Atlantis and in Egypt where I would spend hours just watching the waves of water come in, rolling over one another. This was as good a spot as any to make camp for the night that was coming. I moved back into the trees, finding a spot between bush and grass that was clear for the most part on the ground. Dropping the wood I carried inside the cloth that had covered the body, I began to move the few rocks present out of the area. Looking for fire stone as I did so, finding one piece of it, which I could break into two if needed. I stood back up, setting the fire stone next to the wood pile and looking around for anything that would be edible. Spotting a bush full of berries that birds were perched on, I began walking slowly, trying not to frighten the winged animals. I took one wrong step and a branch that had fallen cracked under my weight, creating a sound that sent the birds into a frenzy, flying every which way and shrieking their calls of warning to the others around. I gave up trying to befriend the animals, gathering berries into the skirt of the dress, along with a few leaves, I picked up the stick I had broken on my way over and went back to the area I had decided to make camp at.

Setting the berries and leaves onto a flat enough rock so they would not roll away, I moved the wood into a small pile, only some of it as it would have to last me through the night. Gathering dry leaves and mixing them into the sticks. I turned on my heels, picking the fire stone up from the ground, striking it against another rock to break it into two pieces. I remembered in Egypt, the friend I had made who was one of the descendants from the people that left Atlantis, they had been the first to show me what fire stone was, insisting on teaching me various plants in the area and the stones that could be used. 'Thank you,' I said allowed, as they had taught me something that I would need on this day. Striking one stone against the other sparks flew from it, reaching the dry leaves and setting fire to them, as they burned hot and red, they began to set the smaller sticks on fire. Which in turn began the larger of them burning, warming the air around me to a tolerable level.

Satisfied with the fire burning in front of me, I sat back, relaxing for a while. Biting into one of the berries it left a bitter, tangy taste on my tongue, almost spitting at that first bite. Once the initial bitterness of the berry died, there was a sweet taste to it. The leaves were not much better, in fact, they were worse, they did not sweeten with time, they remained bitter and sour. But this body had not eaten in some time, it needed the nourishment that the Earth had to offer.

Laying the cloth that the body had been covered in across the ground, I moved a few of the larger wood pieces onto the fire, allowing them to begin to catch the flames before I laid on the cloth. Watching the flames spring up, giving some light as the sun began to set into the western sky. Night came fast, once the sun had begun its descent it seemed to only take a matter of minutes before it was dark. I listened as the calls of the animals died into a whisper around me. I could sense them watching me, but they would not come to me even when I called to them mentally. Finally letting my eyelids drift closed, I blocked out the chill on the air and slept.

Chapter Two

Waking to the sound of voices, I took my time in sitting up, watching the embers of the fire burn themselves out before I pushed myself into a sitting position. Stretching the bones and muscles in the body. The sound of the voices grew louder, it sounded as if someone was arguing with a group of people.

'*Humans.*' I could not believe they could not get along with one another. It was as if they were all mentally challenged, arguing like children all the time. And more times than not the children were better at getting along than the adults were.

I could not take the constant bickering of them any longer. Not only were they loud, but they were scaring the animals in the forest, and the animal I sensed that was near them. '*An animal near them? That meant that one of the animals was not scared of people, that meant someone I could talk to*' I realized, jumping to my feet and looking around to find where they were.

Turning, I saw them in the middle of the field beyond the break of the tree line. The animal held by a rope dangling from it's mouth, it was stomping the ground with one of it's front legs, ears forward, head jostling around. There were three men on one side of it, and a single man on the other side of it. The three on one side, wore clothes, ragged and looked to be in need of a bath from what I could see. And the other, '*by the stars what is he wearing!*' Shiny metal covered his arms, chest, parts of his legs, while a cloth hung from his neck.

Moving out into the field, I hurried to save the poor beast that was in between the men who seemed to have no brain. I could feel the animal was panicked, and agitated at the treatment it was being dealt. Finally noticing that the rope not only came from it's mouth but hung over it's head, as well as having a cloth on it's back, accompanied by an odd object strapped to it. This was unacceptable!

"Enough!" I yelled at the men when I was but a few paces away from them. Each of them stopping the noise they had been making and looking towards me. The hair on my head felt as if it was standing on end, the anger inside building. "Let go of the animal!" I stopped a few feet from the poor beast, who was now looking at me as well. If it had been one of the men, it's mouth, I assumed, would have been hanging open as well from the look in it's eyes.

"And who does ye think she is?" One of the dirty men gave me a dirty look.

"Who I am is not of concern. Let go of the animal!" I took a step towards him.

"Tis ours now. Found him running lose we did." He seemed to puff up his chest like a bird courting another, trying to look bigger.

"Tis not yours, tis no ones if he was loose. And by the sky, what have you done to him!" The animal looked at me again, almost turning it's head to the side, it was confused by my intrusion. The man in the shiny clothes stood in one spot, unmoving, watching me, practically hanging his mouth down to the ground, surprise written across his face.

"Leave before I see fit to make you ours as well." The man

holding the rope to the horse stepped towards me, the other two stepping around to his side.

"Leave the woman be. You may have the horse, but leave her as she is." The shiny clothes wearing one stepped forward, almost in front of me.

"I think we shall take both." The one holding the *horse* as it had been called nodded to the other two.

As the shiny one moved again I noticed the sword at his side, reaching over I grabbed the handle of it, pulling it from the sheath that held it to him.

"Just wait..." He began to say as the sword was pulled from him.

"Let go of the *horse*." I looked at the three of them as the horse took a step backwards, still watching. "Or I will have to remove your hand from him."

The three dirty ones began laughing, stopping a moment in their movement towards me. The shiny one stood beside me, looking at me as if I had grown a second head. The only one present who seemed to have a brain was the horse, who backed another step, pulling the rope at his mouth taunt.

"But my Lady, tis our horse, as you will come as well." The dirty one said again, dropping the rope from his hand and moving with the other two towards me.

I pushed the shiny one beside me with my free hand as I spun the sword at my side. Once again feeling at home, sword in my hand, ready for a fight. I smiled at the dirty ones as one pulled an odd looking knife from his side, it looked to be a mix of a knife and a sword, in between the two in length. The other two pulled knives loose.

Watching from the corner of my eye, I noticed the horse take a few more steps in reverse, still watching the action in front of him with intent interest as the shiny one moved towards me again. "Stay!" Yelling at him, I met his eyes, warning him to stay out of my way. Of which he did not listen, rolling my eyes as I swung the sword at the first of the dirty ones to try to step towards me.

"We do not wish to harm you, but if ye continue such fight we will be forced into it." The dirty one was trying to coax me into submission, the idea of his speech brought a small laugh from me. "Put the sword upon the ground, come easy."

"I say, leave her be." The shiny one again tried to insert himself between me and the others.

"Would you stop with the movement!" I looked at him again. Taking my eyes off of the others, "I do not need thy help, nor do I want it. Be gone!"

Looking away had been a mistake, as one of the dirty ones tried to come up behind me, feeling his energy close to my own I brought an elbow up into the center of his face, sending him backwards as I brought the sword around. Swinging it up from the ground to connect with the knife he loosely held as he fell to the ground. Another, who was moving up behind me came quick, but not fast enough. I brought my arm around, reaching around his neck and bending him backwards, ready to break the bones in his neck in half, as I held the sword straight from my body to the one who ran at me. Stopping just as the tip of the sword met with his neck.

"One should not challenge when one can not fight." I looked at him. Daring him to take that step forward that would embed the tip of the sword into his neck. The one held backwards in my arm was beginning to squirm as I tightened the hold on him. I felt the blade of the knife, he sliced at my leg, dropping him just as it made contact. I brought the sword over my head and down with both hands, severing his hand from his arm. "T'was not a smart move." I looked down at him.

Looking around me, the shiny one stood in shock, staring at me as the two dirty ones backed up and away from me. The one laying on the ground was screaming in agony as he inched away. The horse seemed to be laughing as he nickered, tossing his head up and down. As the one on the ground made his way to his friends, he stood holding his bleeding appendage to his chest. The shiny one stood still, mouth once again hanging open, staring at me. The horse seemed to dance as he made his way over to me, resting the palm of my hand on his forehead, I smiled at him as he jostled his head against me.

Chapter Three

"Good day." I spoke to the horse softly, resting my head against his. He nuzzled his nose against my chest, hanging his head down slightly. I moved my hand up the side of his face, going to remove the rope from around his ears.

"Wait." The shiny one finally moved from his position, stepping towards me.

I turned my head, looking at him. He was not bad for a human, his face was clean of hair, wide shoulders, dark eyes, and dark hair on his head pulled behind him at the nap of his neck. He was tall, if he was right in front of me, I would have had to of looked up to look at him. The shiny metal he wore appeared to be covering cloth.

"What... where..." He stopped, taking a deep breath and looking me over. "What is your name?" He finally managed to speak coherently.

"Nesenty." I told him, shifting my weight from one foot to another, watching him.

"Neenty?" His eyebrows creased on his forehead.

"Knee... sent... ay." I sounded it out for him. The tongue he spoke in was far different from the others I had experienced, I found myself also speaking in it.

"Knee-sent-ay." He sounded it out to himself, then asked, "Where do you hail from?"

"Not of this land." I told him, debating on how much he could handle.

"Where did you learn to use a sword as such?" He looked at the sword, still in my hand, which blood was still dripping from.

"Where I come from." I was growing impatient with him and his interrogation. "You need to learn to use one."

His mouth dropped open yet again as he stared at me. Rolling my eyes, I turned back towards the horse standing next to me. Removing the rope from his head as he nuzzled his nose against my arm. I moved around to his side, finding where the object was tied and undoing it, dumping it from his back.

"What are you doing?" The shiny one moved towards the horse.

"I am removing the obstruction of his body." I turned to face the shiny one, moving between the horse and him.

"He will run if you do such!" He scolded me. Sensing I did not understand his worries he tried to explain, "tis my mount, has habit of running when lose if he is not tied to something. He is young, does not know better."

"Your mount?" I looked from him to the horse who stood still behind me, watching again the interaction between myself and the male of the species.

"My horse. I ride on his back, he takes me where I need go."

"He belongs to none, he is free." I dared him to argue with me.

"Lady, I do not know where it is you come from, but he is of my property, as is the saddle you dumped to the ground." He glared at me, heat rising from his eyes.

"He belongs to none, he will come with me." I lifted the sword, intending on handing it back to the shiny one, "you may have your sword back."

"No, you do not."

"What?"

"You will not take my mount with you." He stepped closer, looking down at me as I glared at him.

He was trying to scare me into submission, of giving the horse behind me to him, again I wondered how the humans had lost their minds. I had just removed the hand of one, proved I could fight and did not scare of the thought of killing and this one challenged me. I heard what sounded like thunder approaching and looked around the shiny ones arm, seeing five more *horses* approaching with shiny people riding on their backs.

"Found your mount did you?" The one in front announced as he came to stop behind the shiny one in front of me.

"Aye, I did." The man in front of me did not stop looking down at me.

"And found woman as well?" The one in front spoke again, chuckling as he did so.

"Aye." He continued to glare down at me.

"Take your sword and be gone." I warned him.

"I will take my mount as well." He moved to go around me.

"No, you will not!" I put my hand on his chest, holding him back as he glared at me. "The horse comes with me."

"Making friends?" Another who rode on a horse began laughing, as did the others mounted on the backs of the animals.

"Looks to be he has come upon a new breed of woman." Another joked.

"She does seem to have no intention of giving his mount back." Another added in.

"Look," Another pointed as he laughed, "she has taken his sword as well."

They were laughing and joking behind his back, at his expense, his face seemed to grow impatient as he glared at me. I could feel the energy coming off him, the anger building in him, glancing down I saw his hands balled into fists at his side.

Moving closer to me, he leaned over, mouth close to my ear, "please, will you return my horse?" He ground out between clenched teeth, soft enough for the others not to hear.

I could feel the horse behind me, wondering what I would do, not afraid of him, seemingly fond of the shiny one in front of me. "If he wishes to go with you." I whispered back.

The shiny one backed a step and whistled, to which the

horse moved out from behind me and stood in front of him. "May I have my sword as well?"

I handed it back to him, watching as he put it back into the sheath at his side. He moved around me, and the horse, going for the *saddle,* as he had called it, lifting it and walking towards the horse. Again the horse moved behind me.

"Horse!" The shiny one hollered at him. "Enough game, come." He stood holding the saddle.

The horses energy felt as if he wanted to be with me, I smiled at the shiny one and shrugged my shoulders. Turning, I walked off a ways, the horse followed, his nose against my back as the shiny one again whistled. A good ten paces away I stopped, turning to face the horse. '*May I ride on you?*' I asked mentally to the horse.

His response was only to nuzzle against me and stand still. I walked to his side and ran my hand along his back. Taking my time in getting up, finally I held the hair of his neck, near his back, swinging myself upwards until I sat on him.

"Horse!" The shiny one yelled again and the horse looked behind him at the man.

The others on top of their horses were laughing, one nearly falling off of his mount during the course of the laughter that rang through them. The shiny one dropped his saddle and came towards us. But before he could reach us, horse began walking off, me upon his back.

Chapter Four

I left the shiny one standing in the middle of the field with the pack of laughing ones, looking back he was standing with his head hung, arms limp at his sides. A twinge of guilt set over as the horse moved further away before stopping. He sensed my indecision over the choices that were being made, looking back as well, I could feel he did not want to leave his friend.

"*Let us go back.*" I mentally connected with him, watching as the shiny one turned around and walked back to his belongings, gathering them up into his arms.

The horse turned and I sensed I needed to hang on, as if he was telling me to hold on. Tightening my legs around his middle and holding onto his neck as he began to pick up the speed with which he traveled, it was a bouncing type of movement.

The laughing ones had begun to turn their mounts around, moving away with the shiny one walking behind them with his belongings in his arms. One of the laughing ones looked back, stopping and turning in his saddle.

"Look!" I heard him tell the shiny one.

He stopped, looking back, watching as horse moved towards him with me on his back. Stopping a few paces away from him. I looked down at him, he seemed to be happy horse had returned, but unsure of me.

"I will return to the fort before the night." The shiny one turned to the others. "Go without me."

"As you wish." One of the laughing ones shrugged, chuckling before he turned with the others, continuing on.

I sat on horses back, looking down at the shiny one as he set his belongings on the ground. Straightening and walking towards us, he watched me carefully, almost as if he was an animal watching me, unsure of approach. Resting his hand on horses nose as horse dropped his head. He looked up at me, still visibly unsure of my intentions.

"My name is William." He offered, finally looking away from me and to horse.

"William." I repeated, making sure I got it correct.

"Aye." He responded softly. "Do you require help down?" Looking back up at me.

"No." I swung my leg over the front of the horse, sliding off his side.

"Where do you reside? I will take you back before returning." He offered to return me from where I came.

"I stayed in the trees night before." I told him, "I can walk back."

His eyes bulged as he looked at me, almost as if he did not believe me. "In the tree?" He repeated, as if he needed to say it aloud before he believed it.

"Aye, right over that way." I pointed to where I had stayed.

"Do you not have home? Family?" He watched me carefully.

"Nay, I do not." I told him, unconcerned.

"Husband?" He asked, watching me with concern written all over his face.

"Nay." I shook my head, trying not to laugh at him.

He looked uncomfortable, shifting his weight, visibly thinking over his options. Concern, worry, along with a variety of other thoughts washed over the look on his face. "How many years are you?" He finally thought of something to say.

"19." I told him the age of the body, not sure he would believe I was as old as I really was.

"Tis not safe for a Lady of your age!" He looked at me, again concern flooding his face.

"How old are you?" I asked, to try and distract him from such thoughts.

"I am 29 years." He responded, almost falling for my change in subject.

"Are you sure tis safe for man of your age to be alone?" I continued to try and distract him.

He laughed, shaking his head as he moved towards his belongings. "A man of my age should have wife and many children running about my legs, not out in middle of the field worrying over some Lady who fights as if she was a man. I have not to worry of myself."

"And yet, your horse was going with three other men and with me?" I challenged him.

"Horse ran when I got off in town, I did not tie him fast enough." He put the rope back on horses head, "he enjoys the playing of games with me." He sat next to his saddle, pulling something wrapped in cloth from a bag at the side of it. "Are you hungry?"

"I have yet to eat this morn." I admitted.

"Come, sit, eat." He stood for a moment, removing the cloth that hung behind him and laying it on the ground, sitting back down and patting it in the signal to sit on it.

Walking over I sat on it, crossing my legs under the skirt of the dress and watching as he unrolled what he had inside. It looked like dried flesh. "What is this?"

"Dried cutting from beef." He looked at me, wondering what I was about not knowing what it was.

"I do not eat meat." I told him firmly.

"You what?" He moved his eyes to look at me as his head was bent towards what sat in his lap, which he was tearing apart.

"I do not eat my animal family. Do you not have vegetation?"

"No." He looked at me, turning his head to match where his eyes looked. "What do you want?" He finally asked, setting the meat down and standing up.

"What do you mean?" I watched him.

"What is it you want to eat? I will go fetch it."

"I will wait until the sun is higher in the sky and get it of my own."

"I can go get such now if you would tell me what you want." He argued with me, growing impatient with me again.

"I do not need your help now as I did not need it before." I stood up, intending on getting my own food.

"Do women always speak as such where you hail from?" He asked genuinely.

"Aye, they do!" I almost yelled at him.

He stood there staring at me as if I had grown that second head again. Standing and staring at one another, I could sense something coming from him. In his eyes he almost had a look of humor in them, the energy coming off of him was of curiosity more so now than aggravation.

Chapter Five

After a time, he began looking me over completely. From my bare feet to my hair, looking the clothes I wore over. "Where are your shoes?" He asked, looking confused.

"I have none." I answered him, unamused at the assessment he was making.

"Robe?"

"What?"

"Something to keep your head warm, like mine that you was sitting upon." He motioned to the cloth laying on the ground.

"Don't have one of those either." I crossed my arms over my chest.

"What do you have?" He asked finally.

"What I wear, a cloth by my camp, some fire stone." I admitted, as barren as it sounded.

"That is it?" He got that expression on his face again, one of concern.

"That is it, and tis all I need." I grew defensive.

"Let us go and get it, then we will return to town." He said, moving towards the saddle that lay on the ground, throwing the blanket on horses back and then the saddle.

"Why?" I didn't understand his actions.

"Because I will not leave my Lady out in the middle of the trees with nothing, to be eaten by bears or ravaged by travelers." He turned away from horse and looked at me.

"I can take care of myself!" I was not about to be treated as a child.

"I can see that." He sighed, "but t'would be dishonorable of me to leave you in such dismay."

"I am not a child, I can care of myself!" I almost stomped my foot glaring at him, to be honest I found this entire situation humorous.

He took a step towards me, putting his hands on my arms and looking down at me, "think of horse, he would worry of you if I left you here. He would run off without me looking for you." He tried to talk me into it.

I looked around him at horse who was standing there, watching me. Rolling my eyes I sighed, "fine. Tis this way." I turned, shrugging his hands off.

Walking towards the tree line, he turned, grabbing the wrapped meat and placing it back into the bag on the saddle, as well as throwing his robe over the saddle and leading horse behind me. I walked into the tree line, making my way to the camp, picking up the cloth and fire stone I had. Turning around I almost collided with William as he was standing behind me, and horse behind him, but I had not heard them approach.

"Sorry my Lady." he swallowed, "was not watching as I walked."

"You are strange." I looked at him before pushing him out of my way.

"Your dress..." He began, following me out of the trees.

"What about it?" I looked back at him.

"Tis untied." He dropped the ropes from horse and moved behind me.

"What are you doing!" I turned around, glaring at him.

"Tying the ends together so your back does not hang out." He grabbed my shoulders and turned me back around. Threading the rope through the holes in the dress and tying it near my neck.

This body was obviously in heat as I could feel the heat from his knuckles on my neck send sparks down my spine. Shaking my head I stepped away mumbling, "thank you."

"You are welcome." His hands dropped down to his sides as he turned and took hold of the rope on horse. Stepping into the loop that hung from the saddle and mounting the horse he moved alongside me, reaching down.

"What?" I looked up at him, not understanding what he was doing.

"I am not going to have you walk to town. How would that look?" He smiled down at me. "Take my hand, I'll pull you up behind me." Reaching up I put my hand in his, swinging up as he pulled me onto horse's rump. "Hang on." He looked back at me.

"To what?" I glared at him as he smiled.

"Around my middle." he reached back, taking hold of my hands and pulling my arms around him.

Horse jumped as William put his heals into his sides. It wasn't the bumpy pace he had gone at before, but a smoother, faster gate. Riding through first the field and then coming to the river, horse slowed a bit as he bounced through the river and hopped up the other side of it, out of the water and onto the opposite bank. Coming out of the bouncy gate he was traveling into a smoother, quicker gate. He veered around trees and continued until I could see the town ahead.

It was not the town this body had come from, thankfully, I did not wish to explain why the body moved again. I felt William pull gently on the rope that was on horse, at the same time horse slowed to a walk.

Riding into the town, I looked at the people, carrying baskets here and there, buildings again of stick and stone, and thatched roofs. Children running around the legs of adults, playing as their parents tried to work around them. Looking up I saw a wall of solid stone pieced together, an opening in the middle of it, and a larger building of pieced stonework ahead. As we rode through the opening, I looked around, seeing smaller buildings of wood and animals around, a man pounding on the blade of a sword with a stone hammer and another placing metal onto a horses foot.

"I see he has gotten his horse." I heard someone say as we came to stop in front of one of the wooden buildings.

"As well as the Lady." Another chuckled.

Looking at them, I recognized them as two of the laughing ones that had been in the field earlier that day. They elbowed each other and seemed to joke with one another.

"You can let go now." William turned in his seat looking back at me.

"Aye, I could." I glared at him. "Where are we?"

"The castle of my Lord." He looked at me, confused again. "You do come from far away do you not."

"I told you I did." I let go of his middle, just in time for him to take hold of my arm as I swung off the back of the horse. Standing on the ground I realized how muddy it was as my feet sunk into it.

"We need get you shoes." He said as he got off of horse, handing his rope to a young boy nearby. "Be sure he is fed well." He ordered the boy who nodded at him.

I could hear the two still joking behind me, turning I glared at them, "what is your problem?"

Pretending to cough they turned their backs to me, trying not to laugh.

"Try not to hold it against them. Not every day they hear a woman speak as you do. They have been drinking wine all morn." William took hold of my arm and led me off a ways. "You may want to watch your tongue, women who speak as you do, most often do not receive a warm welcome. If you do not know how to speak as the other women do, best say nothing at all unless we are alone." He gave me a warning look.

"What is this?" I looked down at the mud I was standing it, it held a stench to it that was unlivable.

"Tis dung, from various animals, mixed with the dirt and urine of them." He laughed at me, "tis why we must get you shoed."

I gagged at the thought of what I was standing it, not only was it smelly but it was unsanitary. "Where do I get shoed and wash'?"

"Come with me, we will find you something. And another dress, perhaps, so you can wear one while you clean the other." He nodded to his right, indicating that I follow him as he turned away.

Following him back outside of the wall and down the hard dirt street, between buildings and markets I looked at the people. They all wore similar clothing, the children ran about clothed, they would look at William but not meet his stare. Coming to a stop in front of me, I bumped into his back. Glancing at me before he moved inside one of the buildings, I waited outside. He returned with an older man who looked me over from head to toe, turning and going back inside, he came out with a dress in hand and a pair of what looked like slippers.

"Should fit'er. If not come back." He handed them to William.

"We will." William handed him coins from a pouch he had at his side. As the older man walked back inside the building, William turned to me. "Now let us go wash your feet, before you put your feet in these." He threw the dress over his arm and hung onto the shoes as he turned and walked off.

Not knowing whether to thank him or yell at him for talking down to me I kept my mouth shut and followed him back inside of the walls. He walked to one of the smaller stone buildings, stepping inside he looked around. "What?" I asked, not realizing what he was doing and why he was not proceeding.

"Everyone out." He ordered and stepped back out of the entry way, I moved as he did as a dozen men left the building. Each of them glancing at me as they left, talking amongst themselves. "You can go in now." He motioned with his head for me to go in.

"Why did you make them leave?" I asked as I walked inside.

"So you could wash, make sure these fit." He held the items up he was carrying. "There is a bucket of water to your left, a fire on the right to dry anything you need to wash." He looked at me, waiting for me to acknowledge what he said, when I did not but stare at him, he explained. "The men do not need inside while you do such. Stay away from the windows if you strip down to your undergarments, I will wait out here."

"What undergarments?" I laughed, knowing very well what he spoke of but wanting to be a pain.

"Dear Lord. We will buy you some of them as well." He hung his head as he shook it.

"No need, I prefer not to have them." I took the dress and shoes from him, turning and walking inside.

"As you say my Lady." He turned around, facing outwards and leaning against the door frame.

"What is it with this Lady this and Lady that?" I asked as I stripped the clothing off.

"What would you have me call you?" He asked.

"Nesenty, my name. I am not Lady." I told him, looking around for a cloth to wash with near the water, finding it and dunking it into the water before beginning to wipe my body off before washing my feet.

"Would be uncustomary to call you by your name only." I heard him sigh, "how about Lady Nesenty?"

"Tis better than nothing." I grumbled. "Why is it uncustomary to call me by my name only?"

"You are not my wife, nor my child, nor my sister." He explained.

"So what do I call you since you are none of them to me?" I asked as I pulled the dress over my head this time.

"Sir William will suffice."

"You can turn around now." I told him once I had the dress on. "Can you tie the back up?"

He turned around slowly, as if to make sure I was dressed before he turned completely around. Walking over to where I stood he looked the dress over, "fits well. Turn around." As I turned he began looping the threads through the holes in the back of the dress, pulling them tight as he did so. Again stopping at the back of my neck and tying it into a loose loop, he stepped back. "Do the shoes fit?"

He nodded, as I looked at him, towards where I had set the shoes. Picking them up I slipped them onto my feet, "fit well enough. But I do not normally wear feet coverings, but as sloppy as it is outside, would be a good idea."

"Unless you care to wash your feet of dung every time you enter a building I suggest you do so." He laughed, "did you wash the dress you were wearing?"

"Was going to, but have not yet." I told him, picking it up and dropping it into the bucket.

"I will see if I can find some vegetation for you since you do not eat meat. Just stay inside here, I will return shortly." He turned to walk out, stopping before he did so, "do not leave here, I will post someone at the door."

"I can care of myself." I reminded him.

He waved his hand and walked out, stopping to talk to one of the men walking by outside who nodded, standing in front of the door way with his back to me.

Chapter Six

He was gone some time, the sun was beginning to set when he finally returned. While he was away it had given me a chance to nose around the building, looking some of the armor and swords over inside of it. The guard standing in the doorway had remained there the entire time, glancing back at me now and then when I would make some sort of noise.

"I apologize for being gone so long." William stepped into the building, relieving the guard he had placed there. "I had a few things to do, I should have brought the vegetation back for you first but truly I got distracted."

He set down a basket full of vegetables and fruits onto one of the beds. Looking it over I made sure there was no meat inside of it, nothing that harmed my senses and smiled at him. "Thank you."

"Ready to see where you will be staying this night?" He asked, picking the basket back up just after I had picked up a piece of fruit out of it.

"I am not staying here?" I looked at him.

He laughed, "not unless you would like to bunk with a room full of single men." He turned towards the doorway, "this way."

Walking outside there were a handful of men sitting on the ground, leaning up against the building, waiting to go inside now that I had exited. Glancing at them as I walked by, following behind William, they wasted no time getting up and going inside.

"Where are we going?" I voiced myself, knowing he meant to take me where I would bunk, but wanting a general idea of where.

"An old shed that holds some things that will be moved on the morrow. I spent most of me time clearing it enough for sleeping this night. I will move it out of the corners in the morn." He stopped, twisting his torso to look back at me, "unless you wish me to do so tonight?"

"You could leave it be, I do not know that I will be staying here." I told him as I came to a stop next to him.

"Where would you go? No family, no husband... I'd rather you be close at hand so I may be at the ready should you need help with something." He began walking again, stopping a few steps away and opening a door, letting me walk through it first.

"You do not have to watch after me." I told him as I went inside. Looking around there was a stack of cloths to my left up against the wall and a pile of straw to my right, in the corner of the building, and a fire had been started dead ahead of me. A window near the straw piled in the corner.

"I cannot disown my vows, protect and help. You may leave, but I would rather I watch over you, keep you safe." He shrugged, setting the basket down on the floor under the window. "There are blankets near the fire, along with wood should it begin to die down tonight."

"I see." I rolled my eyes, my back to him.

"Do you know how to build fire, keep it going?"

"Yes." I turned around and looked at him. "I am quite capable of caring for myself, surprising as it may be."

"Then I will take my leave of you this night Lady, I will return at first light." He backed up to the doorway, holding the handle to the door. "If you need anything, I will be in the barracks, first bed on the left as you come in through the door."

"Uh huh." I watched him for a minute as he debated with himself before closing the door and leaving me there. *Finally... alone,* I thought to myself. Part of me wanting to look out the door to be sure he did not post some man at it, blocking my exit should I decide to leave in the middle of the night. *If I do decide to leave, I can always render that guard unconscious, but might as well take shelter as long as I have it.* I moved over to the straw, throwing myself down into the middle of it and picking up a vegetable, snacking on it as I watched the fire begin to dwindle down. Standing up, I threw one of the larger logs onto it, moving it around with a stick to get oxygen to the flames. Straightening myself I picked up a blanket, satisfied the fire would burn itself out and heat the room for the night, I laid on the straw, pulling the blanket over me and relaxing into sleep as the moon made it's presence known out the window.

Chapter Seven

The next morning I woke to find William standing in the doorway, watching me as I laid in the straw, sprawled out with the blanket barely covering me. He stood there, arms crossed over his chest leaning against the door frame, lacking the shiny metal coverings, just a white shirt and brown pants, and a pair of boots. He looked more like a human now, I smiled at the idea.

"Your fire went out." He stated the obvious as he stepped away from the frame, dropping his arms to his sides.

"It did." I yawned as I stretched the body, feeling the straw poking into my back as I did. He stood there, just watching, he seemed to have a habit of watching people. "Yes?" I asked, not being able to stand the way he was staring at me any longer.

"Hm?" He shook his head.

"Can I help you?"

"Ah... no, sorry." He coughed, turning his gaze in a downward direction.

Standing up, I stretched again, the body had knots in it that needed to be worked out. "Is there a relief station near by?" I asked.

His head coming up from the downward gaze. "Oh," as if

what I had asked just struck him, "yes. Is around the corner. When you step outside, go to your right, around the building, you'll see the wooden building there."

"Uh huh." I mumbled as I walked past him, finding my way around to where the building was. It was more of a shack, wooden planks nailed together and stood up for sides, with a grass roof covering it, a door that hung slightly off the hinges. The smell inside was horrid, staying as little time as I had to I left the building, going back around to the doorway of the building I had stayed in before. Stopping in the entry way and watching as William scurried about the room, picking cloths up from one area and turning towards the doorway where I stood.

"I... ah... I will finish cleaning up now, if you do not mind?" He stumbled over his words, arms full of cloths that needed mending. Waiting for me to approve.

Shaking my head I closed my eyes, "if you want to." I stepped back out of the doorway, letting him pass.

He carried the cloths over to the barracks, going inside and coming out without them in his arms and returning to where I had sat on a stone outside of the building. Looking down at me before going back inside, again carrying an arm full of cloth out and into the barracks. He made one more trip, clearing the room of all of them. Coming out of the barracks this time, he went to another building, bringing a few boys with him carrying large baskets that were half their own size, a shovel in his hand.

The boys lined up with the baskets near the doorway, one standing just inside of it as William began shoveling the straw and dumping it into the basket. As the first was filled the boy left with it and the second one took his place. William continued to fill that basket and the third stepped up to take his place, just as the first one returned with his empty basket. They switched positions again and the second boy returned. They continued to rotate positions, filling basket after basket and carrying them to the building that horse had gone into.

"That is it." William stepped out finally, shooing the boys off with the baskets and shovel he had used.

Peeking around the corner of the frame I saw the room clear of cloth and straw, a hard wood floor, the fire wood still there, the blankets folded and set beside it. "Now where do I sleep?" I laughed, he had removed what I had used as a bed the night before.

"Just wait here." He looked down at me, walking towards the barracks and returning with an odd object. It looked as if straw had been tied onto the end of a branch.

He went back inside of the building and began a sweeping motion with it, clearing the room of dust and brushing it out of the door. Leaning the object against the wall he left the building again, going into the building that horse had gone into.

I stood up, looking the room over and taking my shoes off at the door, setting them down before I stepped inside. I looked the room over, he had cleaned it. The wood on my feet felt firm, clean of pebbles and dirt. Squatting down I looked the object he had used over, it was indeed a form of straw tied together and then tied to a smoothed branch.

"Look out." I heard William's voice, looking up I saw a huge form of nailed wood. Almost as wide as the doorway. Stepping back out of the way as he twisted it from side to side, moving it slightly to make it fit between the frame of the door. It scrapped the wood flooring as it came, making an awful sound as it did so. Just past the door frame he glanced around to make sure I wasn't standing in front of it and then tipped it over onto it's side. With a crashing sound it hit the floor and fell over on its side. Four legs on the floor, a rectangular frame on top of them and wooden sides on top of that. With more planks of wood crossing over the middle of it. Bending slightly, he pushed on the side closest to him, pushing it up against the wall the straw had sat in.

Brushing his hands off as he stood straight up again, he turned and left the building. Stepping behind him until I was in the doorway I watched as he went into the same building again, coming out of it a few moments later with a bed under his arm.

"Excuse me..." He said as he came a few feet from the doorway, I back and moved out of the way as he came inside. Throwing the bed on top of the wooden frame and adjusting it until it fit between the sidings of the frame. He moved towards the fire, picking the blankets up and unfolding one, laying it smoothly over the top of the bed, tucking it's ends under the edges between the bed and frame. The other he left folded and set at an end. Standing back he looked it over before turning and leaving again, this time going into the barracks and returning with what looked like a headrest, which he placed at the other end of the bed. "Done." He turned towards me.

"What are you doing?" I asked, pretty sure of what he was doing, but wanting confirmation that I assumed correctly.

"Making the area livable for you." His brows creased as a few lines formed on his forehead.

"Huh." I mumbled.

"Does it not suit you?" He watched me move and run my hand over the bed.

"Suits me fine, as did the straw I slept on night before." I looked at him.

"This will be more comfortable than having straw dig into your back all night."

"I assume it will."

"Do you require anything else?" He stepped away, grabbing the object leaning against the wall and sweeping again at the floor, removing the dirt he had tracked in.

"No. Thank you." I choked out between my teeth.

"Wait here until I return from this mornings duties. Then I will take you into town, see if we can't find anything that meets your pleasures." He nodded at me as he stepped outside, leaning the object against the inside wall as he did so.

"Alright." I moved towards the door, intending on slamming it on him for trying to confine me to the room.

He acted as if he had read my mind and put his hand against the door, "please do not disappear, I do not want to spend my day trying to find you."

"I will be here until you return." I gagged on my agreement as I pushed the door closed, turning and dropping myself onto the bed. Elbows on my knees with my chin resting on my hands.

Chapter Eight

Sitting there, the room seemed to be beginning to close in on me. Being stuck in the building was not something I enjoyed. Standing up, I paced around the room, checking the walls for cracks or knots in the wood. Kneeling onto the bed I looked the window over, with no one around I didn't see any harm in creating a cover for it.

Closing my eyes, I concentrated on a cloth I had picked up from the end of the bed, imagining nails as were used on the rest of the building in the ends of it, securing it to the top of the frame in the window. When I opened my eyes, it was a cover that could be moved aside or left to hang over the opening. Sitting back down on my heels on the bed, I let the body dump itself over sideways and laid on the bed, staring up at the roof for some time.

Having had enough of laying around, I stood, picking up a vegetable out of the basket at the foot of the bed, moving towards where the fire had been and looking it over. Counting the blades of dry grass in the pile nearby, along with the sticks and logs that sat in separate piles as well. Moving back by the bed, I sat with my back to it, legs crossed under the dress, resting the backs of my hands on my knees. *No reason I need to go mad sitting here* I decided, closing my eyes and leaving the physical form I occupied. Viewing the room from the mind's eye I moved towards the door, picturing myself outside as it came into my view.

Looking around me there were people, mainly men, moving

about the area. In and out of buildings, this way and that way. Children who seemed to be about 10 or 11 coming and going from the building horse had gone into. Making my way over and into the building, there were smaller sections inside which had a horse in them, small doors on the front, gates to keep them in. The horses were either hanging their heads out, standing inside, or munching on greens that had been thrown into the pens. There was an opening at the other side of the building, much the same as this side, almost as if a large square had been cut out of the middle of it. The roof was solid wood, no thatched grass covering it. Saddles and ropes for the heads hung on what seemed to be branches protruding from the wood walls next to the gates of each pen, along with blankets similar to that of the one horse had, had draped over them.

    Walking out the other opening I saw a larger area, with wooden planks nailed together making a fence around it, a gate at the closest end. Men were riding horses, turning them this way and that, as if teaching the horses to listen to signals they gave them. A few of the horses seemed downright stubborn as they would yank away from a mans hold on the rope, turning another direction before kicking their feet up. There was one at the other end of the pen, who stood on the ground staring right at a man, almost face to face with each other, like they were trying to back the other down. The horse moved slightly, kicking it's front leg out and striking at the man who jumped out of the way.

    Turning away from the view, I noticed that to the right of it there was a smaller area, where a few boys stood with wooden training swords in their hands. An instructor in front of them with another of the training weapons, showing them movements. It seemed a little rough, uncoordinated almost, as if the man knew how to use a sword but not with easy movements. Shaking my head I walked in the other direction, finding a larger fenced in area with poles driven into the ground in some areas, with rings hanging down from an offshoot that stuck out to the side. Men riding horses inside of it, carrying large branches of wood under their arms. One rode at a quick pace down it, threading the branch he carried through the rings.

"...Nesenty?" I heard the voice, muffled as it was.

Opening my eyes, I was back in the physical body, William squatting in front of me, his face practically right in front of mine. I glared at him, only a few inches away from me, his hands on my shoulders as if he had been shaking me.

"Are you alright my Lady?" He turned his head to the side.

"I was." I responded.

"Why do you sit like this with your eyes closed? And did not respond when I came in?"

"I was..." I tried to think of a way to explain it so he would understand, "...resting my eyes, ignoring the things around me." I lied through my teeth to him, he wouldn't understand what I was doing even if I could explain it to him.

"If you say so." He stood up.

"Where are your boots?" I asked, noticing his feet were bare of the boots and covered in cloth instead.

"Did not want to track muck into your room, they are just outside the door." He laughed as if it was apparent.

I glared up at him, holding my mouth tightly shut. Not at all happy with the intrusion while I was just getting to look around the area. He did nothing but stare down at me. "Do you want something?"

"I am finished for this morn, came back to see if you had want to go into the town. Found you sitting as if you were sleeping upright." He shrugged, stepping towards the door, glancing back, "well? Do you want to?"

"Might as well, better than being stuck in here." I stood up, straightening the skirt of the dress with my hands. I moved over to the doorway, pulling my shoes on as he put his feet back inside of the boots he wore. Stepping outside the sun had risen to almost the middle of the sky already.

"As soon as you are acquainted with the area you can come and go as you please, but I do not want you getting lost." He reached around, pulling the door closed behind me.

"I have a better sense of direction than to get lost." I looked up at him standing next to me.

"You may, but still will ease my mind if I show you about first." He moved away, walking towards the opening in the stone wall. I followed behind him, looking around at the surroundings, the people inside of the walls.

Chapter Nine

Once outside the wall the surroundings seemed to be busy with activity. Men and women, as well as children every direction you looked. People of all ages doing various tasks, selling various items of different sizes, colors, textures, forms. Following behind William as he went to the right on the hard dirt road I found myself in the center of the activity, people making deals over items and coins of silver and gold being exchanged.

Stopping at one of the tables I was attracted to a chain with a golden figure on it that had, in the exact center of it, a crystal type of stone in it. Picking it up and turning it, it caught the light, shimmering in different colors. Looking closer at the golden figure, it has a woman's form, bare, cut off at the legs and shoulders, with her stomach rounded. The stone embedded into her chest between the breasts which were plump. The back of the figure was flat and at the top there was a small hole with a ring of gold color run through it that attacked it to the silver chain. Looking at the other items that laid on the table there was another silver chain that held a crystal attached to it by a silver cap that pressed into the stone around the top, again with a small ring at the top which hung from the chain. It reminded me of the crystals we had worn in Atlantis.

"Where did this come from?" I asked the man standing behind the table.

He looked at me as if I should have known, pausing and

looking at the item I held in my hand and then back at me. "I crafted it."

"But where did the crystal come from?" I wanted to know if it had been passed down in his family, if he could be a descendant from someone I had once known.

"I found it, a large chunk of it in the hills. Cut and shaped it into what you see now." He explained. "The silver of the chain and top are from a cave not far from here, where most of the silver you see around is mined out of."

"Do you like it?" William was standing next to me.

"It reminds me of the crystal I once wore." I nodded at him.

"How much?" He asked the man behind the table.

"A single mark of silver." The man smiled. "Suits your Lady I think."

William nodded, pulling the pouch he had taken coins from the day before out and removing a silver coin with a figure engraved on it and handing it to the man. Turning towards me he reached for the crystal, "turn around."

I let him take it and turned around as he had requested, feeling his hand move the hair out of the way before he reach above my shoulders, lowering the crystal in front of me and pulling the chain around the back of my neck. Hooking it together and straightening it along my neck, he moved my hair back where it had been. I looked down at it, not quite understanding why he had exchanged one round piece of silver for this, as I had no concept of money. But I liked the energy that came from the crystal. It had a natural, easy energy to it, something that seemed to connect to the earth.

"Looks well on her." The man behind the table said before he turned and went to speak to someone else.

"That it does." William voiced as I turned around. "Like it?"

"Mhm." I nodded, glancing at him as I fiddled with the crystal between my thumb and finger. "Why did you give him that silver coin?"

He laughed, "because you must pay for items you want." He looked at me, realizing I was serious, "do they not pay for items where you come from?"

"In a way, I think it could be considered payment." Thinking of a way to explain it before I opened my mouth again. "Where I come from, most things are given. You work, you take a portion and you use it, or you trade it for something else that you need... or want."

"Well, I traded that silver coin for the necklace you wear now." He paused, sighing, "think of it like this. You want, or need, something in this town, you trade silver or gold coins, depending on the price the crafter has set. They give it to you, you give them that. The coins allow them to purchase food, pay tax, buy wood if they do not cut it themselves, clothes."

"Tax?" I asked as we started walking.

"Coins paid to his Lordship, our King, for his protection as well as letting them live on his land." William explained as he traded another coin with someone selling dried flesh.

"His land? But the earth belongs to no one." I argued.

"You are strange my Lady. The land you see around you, as far as you can see, belongs to our King. He asks people to trade in coins for living on it, building homes, having families, working it."

"Why?" I didn't understand their ways, it seemed a rotten way to live.

"Because... is how it works. Always has." He shrugged his shoulders looking down at me.

"Not always." I mumbled.

"And in turn for living on his land, they are benefited his protection." William ignored my comment, "if war happens, they are brought inside the walls and remain there while people, such as myself, drive the offenders away."

"That should be free." I commented. "Should be expected of a King, not bought with *tax*, he should do it freely out of the kindness of his heart."

William stopped at the end of the street, turning and looking at me, "is that how it is where you are from?"

"Yes. And if it is not even our people, our King takes others in. Feeds them, clothes them, gives them house to live in, protects them, and does not ask for coins of silver and gold!"

"Hm..." he responded, mulling over the idea before pointing to a large building with lots of windows in it that men were coming and going from, "that building. Do not go in, you will not like what you find."

"Why?" I was curious now, he should not have told me not to go in, it only raised my interest in it.

"Because it is a woman's home. Also sells ale and wines inside of it." He noticed my expression of confusion and went on, "the women in there, they see to the needs of a man. Are paid well for it I might add. If you go in there, chances be that you would find yourself receiving coins from a man with ideas in his head of..." he choked on what he was going to say and replaced it with something else, "...taking you to a room alone."

"So the women trade favors to a man for coins?" I clarified.

"You may call them that, yes." He nodded, pointing to another building. "There they serve food, table and chair inside for sitting. Wine, ale, water with plates of meat and very few vegetables. You may not like the food inside of there."

"And again you trade coins for this?"

He laughed, "yes. And there," he pointed to another, smaller building, "you may find a seamstress, if needed to make the clothes you wear smaller or larger. Over here," he nodded to the building my dress had come from, "the man and his wife make clothes for both men and women, as well as children. And the markets along these streets hold various items like you were looking at and more, along with a few places that have vegetation from the surrounding land that is brought in."

"What is beyond these streets?" I wanted to know.

"Homes, families." He shrugged again, "some are smaller versions of the woman's house, one or two women living and seeing to men on a smaller scale."

"How many people live around here?"

"Hundreds. Maybe more. Never stopped to count." He glanced down as we came back to the end of the street where we had started. "If you take this road out, and go to your left, you will find fields of barely and hay. Where the road breaks, if you go to your right, you will find trees with fruit that is brought in and vines that grow grapes and other berries. And further down from the break in the road, you will find other fields with vegetables growing. And beyond that there are other areas where other things are grown, as well as animals that are brought to slaughter when they come to age."

"And people work those fields and bring it in?" I asked.

"Yes, they are paid in a share of it, which they may sell or use for their families."

"What happens to the rest of it, that is not paid to them?"

"Given to the King and his family. Passed out among those of us who work for him." He seemed accepting of how things worked.

"And those buildings?" I pointed to the ones that were to the left of the entry of the wall.

"More homes, more families. Behind them is a small wall that is still being built. Masons work on it, are extending it around the entire town."

"Where do you get the coins you carry?" I was wondering if he worked for any of them.

"Paid from the taxes, our Lord collects, to us. For our

services to him and his family."

"I have yet to see you work." I commented on the fact all I had seen him do so far is sleep, order people around and clean.

Laughing he looked at me, "I am on hand should he need something. At the ready to take my horse and drive offenders out of his land. I train horses, as well as help with the training of squires."

"What's a squire?" I asked.

"Like the boys who helped with the removal of the straw. Young boys, or young men, who wish to serve our King one day."

"So you are like a bodyguard?" I finally put the idea of what he was explaining together with what I did.

"Kind of, yes." He nodded, "one of many who form an army of sorts."

"So your King, and his family, are that..." I tried to think of the word to explain it, "...they get into enough situations, trouble, that they require an entire army to stand over them?"

"It is more of they could be attacked and it requires many of us to escort them or watch over their lands. Not so much that they put themselves into positions of trouble." He began walking back inside of the wall again. "Over here," he pointed to the building the horses were in, "is where we keep out mounts when they are not loose in a pasture. Keeps them dry and available if we need them."

"Do they not get tired of the confines?" I asked as we started walking that way.

"Yes, which is why we turn them out into pasture some days, let them run off their energy some." We walked into the building and headed for the other opening, "outside of here you will find training areas. We train young horses to be ridden right outside. And to the right we train the squires when they are not seeing to other duties. And to your left we keep our own skills honed. Beyond here there is an arena where competitions are held." He turned and headed back the other way.

"Competitions?" I did not understand his terminology.

"When festivities are held, we put on a show. Sometimes squires who have completed their training are involved, if they show promise they are knighted in the evening after the festivities by the King." He stopped when we exited the building, "that building is called the stables. The building I stay in is one of the four barracks you will find in the area. And if you follow this road straight up to the next stone wall, you will find the castle where the King and his family stay. Along with anyone they have that are visiting from another land."

"Are all the men who work here single?" I had yet to see any family groups.

"No, the married men live in homes, not barracks. Tis back beyond the building you occupy. There are many homes that direction, near the outside wall. Along with another market where some of the food is stored and sold, or given." He pointed to one of the streets, "if you find yourself in need of food or fresh water, you can take that street down and find the markets that direction. Tell them I sent you and they will give you what you need."

"And the man that was sitting outside the walls?" I asked about the older man I had seen sitting against the wall on the outside.

"Is poor... he is too old to work and no family to care of him." William shrugged, not the least bit concerned, "he collects coins or food people give to him. Uses it to pay the tax that the King collects, sometimes buys food or leather."

"Why does your King not take care of him?" I didn't see why they let the old man live like he did.

"Because is not our Lord's fault he has no family and cannot work."

"But it is one of his people, should he not build him home or feed and cloth him? Is not the mans fault that he has no family either, is not his fault he has aged." I was beginning to grow angry at the treatment.

"That is not how it works here, I cannot change it." He gave me a dirty look for the scolding tone I had used in reference to his King.

"Fine." I looked away, not wanting to bite his head off for things he couldn't control.

"Will you be alright for this afternoon?" He softened his tone and facial expression, "I have a few things to do, but I will meet you tonight and join you for sup if that is alright?"

"I will be fine and that is fine by me also." I shrugged, stepping towards the door to my building.

"Be easy and take care, do not wonder too far away." He chuckled, turning away and heading for the stables.

"Thank you for the crystal." I called after him, to which I only received a wave of his hand.

Chapter Ten

That night he showed up just as the sun was setting, cooked vegetables in one bowl and raw fruits in another. "Since you do not eat meat." He shrugged as he came in.

"Does this mean you give up meat as well?" I smiled, trying to put that seed of thought into his head.

"Just for this night." He laughed. "What did you do this evening after I left?" He sat on the floor, back to my bed with his legs crossed, handing a bowl up to me as I sat on the bed.

"Stared at the walls." I popped one of the berries into my mouth.

"Did not see fit to go out, explore?"

"No, I will do that on the marrow when I have all day."

"If you would like, I can go with after my morning duties are completed." He offered.

"Or you can take care of them while I explore around where you are." It was of more interest to me to see what he actually did than to be shadowed by him as if he was watching a child.

"When would you like me to wake you?" He looked up.

"When do you start?"

"I begin before the sun rises. I can break and wake you after it has risen." He was trying to be polite.

"I am normally up long before the sun says good day to the world." I shrugged, smiling, "would you like me to wake you when I rise?"

"If you manage to rise before me, you may wake me." His tone gave away his inner thoughts, he thought I was joking him, he did not believe for one second that I rose as early as I claimed, even though it was probably because I most often drifted back into a sleep state from boredom and he found me asleep most mornings.

"We shall see then." I nudged his shoulder, exchanging the bowl of fruit for the vegetables he had in his hand.

Finishing our meal, we said good night and he left the building as I was stirring the logs in the fire around. Crawling into bed, I watched the ceiling, pulling the curtain away slightly and looking out at the stars for a while before falling asleep.

The following morning, when I woke the first time, I pulled myself up out of bed. It was still dark out, the sun had not even began to show as the Earth had not rotated far enough. Pulling my shoes on I slipped silently out of the building, making no noise as I crossed to the barracks. I slipped the shoes off as I stepped inside, my bare feet against the hard wood floors.

Silently inching my way over to his bed, I watched for a moment as he slept, debating on the waking I should give him. It was either shake him, push him off the bed, or pounce on him.

Smiling at the idea of how he would react to any of those, I couldn't help taking the later choice which would shake him, and more than likely cause him to fall off the bed. As well as wake the rest of the men in here.

Inching slightly, without noise I lowered my left knee onto the side of his bed, watching him move slightly but not waking. Without any further attempts at not waking him, I plopped myself onto his bed, almost sitting on top of him.

His reaction was as expected, first his eyes shot open without seeing as he grabbed for the sword that rested near the head of his bed. As he reached, he grabbed a hold of my neck, pulling me with until we both fell from the bed. The entire building was up in arms as we hit the floor, I was laughing hysterically as he knelt above me, the look on his face was priceless as he was ready to fight but could not understand why I was there.

"The call of waking." I smiled at him as I continued to laugh.

The man who bunked next to him leaned over the side of his bed, and grumbled at us, "as pleasant as it may be to watch what you are doing. Do you see fit to take it to another location, I still have rest to get."

William still held a look of waiting for someone to attack, staring at me. He had let go of my throat when he had seen it was me, but his body posture and the tension I felt from him told me he was waiting for the rest of whatever army was present to jump him.

"By God man! To her room with you!" One of the others hollered as they lay back down.

"Aye!" Another pipped in, "if you are going to make such noise with your activities, need not be in here!"

"What are you doing?" William whispered as he sat back, his backside on my legs and knees beside them.

"You said to wake you when I rose." I smiled, trying to contain the laughter bubbling to the surface.

"Did you stay awake all night?" He moved, standing up and getting his weight off of my legs.

"No. This is just when I rise the first time." I took the hand he offered as he pulled me to my feet. "You find me in the mornings when I allow myself to drift off to sleep again." I brushed the skirt down so it would not be riding up my legs any longer.

"Go outside, I will be there in a moment." He grumbled, turning away from me and reaching for his shirt.

I did such, laughing the entire way as the other men who bunked grumbled as they turned their backs towards the doorway, and me. Every one of them had been awakened, and every one of them was expecting a fight only to find me. How disappointed they must have been, *I must do this more often* I thought to myself, smiling as I pulled my shoes on and stepped from the doorway.

Chapter Eleven

Waiting outside, it was only moments before he came from inside the building, sword belted around his hips, knife in a pouch at his back, lacking any shiny metal coverings. Rubbing his face he came to a stand still beside me, "you ready?"

"Have been ready since I woke." I gave him a look, trying to contain the laughter from the image of his face when he first awoke.

"First the stables, thanks be to you, the boys there are woken earlier than normal." He looked at me as he walked off for the building that held the horses.

"I am sure they will lay blame on you." I told him in a giddy tone of voice, still laughing inside from the previous events.

"I am sure they will as well, as they did not see you jump me."

"I could not resist. You said to wake you when I woke, and you looked ready to be jumped laying there."

Shaking his head as he dropped it down slightly, "I would much prefer the jumping not to take place in front of my men. You do not know them as I do, they will assume things..." He let it trail off, not finishing what he was going to say.

"They will assume no matter what, the mans mind works that way." I told him which only offered me a quick glance from him, almost as if he was shocked I would say something so crude.

We entered the stables, going into a room at this end of it which now held the straw that was removed from my room, as well as bunks with boys bedded down in them. "Tis time to wake!" William's voice rose as he stepped towards one of the bunks, knocking it with his hand, as well as each of the other bunks. Waking each boy up, making sure they were getting out of their beds. "Dress yourselves and come out." He ordered, staring at me to move out of the room.

"And you think I woke you rudely?" I almost laughed.

"I would have preferred that waking... I can let you wake them next time if you wish. But I do not think they will respond as well to being jumped upon." He shook his head as he saw the smile come across my face.

One by one the boys came out of the room, looking around. "But Sir, the sun is not even beginning to rise?" The eldest looking one of them stated as they formed a line down the side of the wall.

"Truthfully I know this... was not my decision." William glared at me. "We start early today."

Looking the boys over, it seemed they had lined up with the youngest to the inside of the building and the eldest towards the outside. "Are they not a little young?" I leaned towards William, asking in a low tone.

"They are of age enough." He gave me a look that was meant to silence me.

"But that one," I pointed to the littlest one, "looks only near 5 or 6 years?"

"7... and he is old enough." He glared at me again, "today we are showing our Lady the trade which we do. Who wants to explain what we do first?" William turned back to the line of boys.

Looking at one another as if they were confused by the event, the eldest stepped forward first. He had to be 14 or 15 by his size. "First we clean the stalls that the horses are in my Lady. We clear it of the dung from over night before we feed them so it does not sour their food."

"Good memory." William nodded at him, "now see to it."

The boys all began scurrying about the building, going into a room across the hall from theirs and coming out with shovels in their hands, entering stalls. The boys began cleaning each one, even the smallest of the boys. I was watching him as William walked around checking on the others. The little one came to just above the knee of the horse who was in the stall with him. He had no fear of the horse as it nosed him. Shovel after shovel of horse manure was thrown out of the gate, and the horse took notice that the gate was open. Moving towards it the little boy saw him, dropping the shovel he ran around in front of the horse and just as I thought he would get walked over, he grabbed the horse by the nostril, pulling it's head down to look him in the face.

"No! Bad horse!" He pointed his little finger at it, "in with you!" The horse looked at him, it's eyes big and watching. Turning it went to the back of it's stall, allowing the child to finish clearing it of the dung from over night.

"He only cleans this one," William stood next to me, leaning on the open gate, "the others clean the rest of them in the time it takes him to clear this one. If you were wondering if I made him work like a man."

"The horse seems to listen to him." I commented on the exchange I had just seen.

"Is an older horse, we keep him in for working with the young children. Does not have so much as one bone in his body that would hurt a child." He chuckled, "would let them hang from his ears and tail if they chose to do such. But he does keep them paying attention to their surroundings, if they seem to forget he is there he bites them in the rump."

As the child came out of the stall he looked up at me, watching me for a moment before setting his shovel back inside of the room it had come from. Lining up against the wall with the others that had done so as the eldest of them loaded the piles outside of the stalls into a bucket on wheels. After it was pushed outside he joined the others in the line.

"What do we do next?" William turned towards them.

"What do you mean we?" I looked at him, "so far I have seen you do not but watch them."

He glared at me as the boys began chuckling, trying to keep the smiles from their faces. "Who wants to explain this to the Lady?"

"He... does not, as you said, because tis our job, we must earn our keep." The second one in line from the eldest boy offered. "He watches to see that it is done correctly, and shows us the correct way to do such if we take a misstep."

"Correct Squire John." He gave me another dirty look

before turning his gaze back on the line of boys, "and what do *we* do next?"

"We feed the animals of course. They may not work on empty stomachs." The same boy offered again.

"No waiting for them to feed themselves now." William announced as the boys jumped to work. Hurrying down to the other side of the building and entering a room at that end, the smaller ones carrying buckets out and the older ones working together to lift round, ball shaped bales out of the room before breaking them open at the end of the building.

"You keep asking such questions, and I may find a mind to put you to work as well." William nudged my arm.

"Ha ha... I would like to see you make me work while you did not but stand around." I gave him a look. "What tis in the buckets the small ones carry?"

"Oats." He looked down at me, "is easier for them to carry, gives them a mind to stay out of the pen when tis feeding time as the horses love it. May run them over if they were to walk inside with it in their hands."

The little one was again at the gate to the stall he had cleaned before, trying to reach his little arms over the side as the horse waited, growing impatient but not moving from his spot. "Come on now!" The little one was on his tiptoes reaching over the side of the gate.

"Are you going to help him?" I glared at William.

"No! I do my own!" The little one turned and gave me a dirty look as the horse grabbed the edge of the pan he held. It was a surprise to watch the horse seemingly dump it into a trough that was inside of his stall before bunting it with his nose back over the side of the gate. It landed atop the child's head as he giggled and ran back down the stables.

"He does not want my help," William shrugged, smiling at me, "and it seems the horse did not have a mind to wait for him to climb the side today."

"You oaf." I pushed his arm this time.

Turning my gaze back down the stables the boys carried arms of green hay down the rows to each stall, dumping it over the side of the gate into the troughs that were in there. Closing the door to the room they had been in they came to stand in the line again.

Chapter Twelve

"What do we do next?" William looked at the boys.

"Sir, we practice... but... the sun is barely up?" The eldest of them looked at him.

"Sometimes we must do things whether it seems time to or not. Does not matter if it is middle of the night, or middle of the day." He was trying to use my waking him early in two ways, one as a learning experience for the boys, and second to make me feel guilty for getting them up so early. The later of which he would have no luck with. "Go ready yourselves, I will be along momentarily."

The boys all went down to the other end of the stables, into the room across the hall from where the food had been, carrying different, proportional sized training weapons with them, and went out the other end. The littlest one of them had a wooden sword that was the length of his leg, from his foot to his hips, which he waved about his head.

"You train them?" I smiled at William. "Lot of good t'will do them, I had to take your sword to get your horse back."

"I let you take my sword." He nudged me. "Try not to give the boys any more ideas by lashing your tongue about your mouth like you did in here."

"Uh huh..." I pushed him as we walked down the stables, coming out and heading to our right where the older boys were already pairing off, leaving the littlest one running up to William.

"You ready?" William looked down at the little one who only nodded. Turning his gaze back on me, "you can go if you would like, or sit somewhere."

"I think I will stay. Must be a humorous event to watch you hurt yourself." I smiled at him as he glared at me. Stopping and sitting down on one of the straw piles as he went with the little one, still waving his sword around and clunking anyone near by who did not move quick enough.

William picked up a wooden sword from one of the older boys and took a stance, one foot in front of the other. Of which the boys copied, all the swords held pointing at the ground, both hands on the handle of it. Giving them instruction as he seemed to move through the motions of using a sword.

The older boys broke off after a bit, putting some distance between themselves and others. Sparing with one another, if that is what you could call it. The little one sliced at William's knees and then his torso, playing along William acted wounded, dropping his sword and falling to his knees as the little one took another swing at his arm, knocking him over. Once laying on the ground the little one finished by putting the tip of his little wooden sword into where William's heart would be. Laughing as he stood up he patted the little boy on the head who jumped around, this way and that, giggling as he did so.

"You want to try?" William stopped in front of me, looking down at me.

"You sure you will not get harmed?" I thought his

instruction was lacking, the boys still had jerky movements, unbalanced strikes, and they never once used physical contact besides the swords striking another.

"You are a woman, what do I have to fear?" He smiled at me, trying to goad me into it.

"Real blade or wooden ones?" It worked, I was not about to back down to someone with barbarian tactics.

"Wood..." He smiled at me, handing the one he had been using to me, "...do not want you losing your pretty little hands."

"I think your more worried about yourself." I poked him in the back as he turned around.

"Sword John!" He hollered at the older boy as they came in from where they were. Tossing the sword he held to William, the boys plunked down on the straw. "Everyone remain out of the way, we do not want to distract the Lady and have her get harmed."

I smiled as his back was still turned to me, I brought the sword to sit against his neck. "Your dead."

"We had not started yet." He turned around and looked at me.

"You made your first mistake, there is no start to a fight, only an end. And now I have your head because you turned your back to me." I was going to enjoy this, not only would I prove yet again I could fight, but his boys would be giving him a time about it for a while.

"But for the purpose of training, we use a start and finish." William moved over to where the boys had been. "Take your guard and defend against an attack." He assumed that foot in front of the other position again with his swords tip touching the ground, both hands on the handle.

Shaking my head, I bent over, tying the skirt of the dress up a ways so it would not tangle between my feet, assuming a much different position than him. I spread my legs, turned so I was sideways, my front leg stretched out, my back leg bent at the knee so the thigh was straight to the ground. My right hand holding the sword up above my head, bent at the elbow the sword was straight with the ground. My left hand in front of my chest. I smiled at William as he looked sideways at me.

Moving towards me he brought his sword up, leaving his entire body open as he did so. Sliding a foot around, I moved to the side, bringing my elbow that held the sword into his stomach as he brought his sword down where I had been. "Must not leave yourself open." I whispered to him as he bent over slightly, catching the breath I had knocked out of him. I brought the sword around to his back, laying it against him, and whispered again, "and do not stop to breathe or you may lose your life." I had wounded his expectations of me, he expected me not to fight, and now he had looked a fool in front of the boys. He was not pleased at all as he straightened himself, bringing the blade of his sword around towards me. Jumping back I spun the sword around at my side and smiled at him for missing me. As he moved towards me, I finally engaged him, bringing the sword I held up from beside me to connect with his as he brought it down. Twisting my body as I turned I brought my elbow into him again, "one must fight, not only with the weapon, but with the rest of their body." I tilted my head to smile at him.

This time he came at me, in a full on attack, knocking me back with his mere size put behind the blow. He almost looked sorry as he mouthed something at me as I lay on the ground.

Coming towards me, I assumed he meant to help me up, but instead I put my hands next to my head and forced my body upwards, leaving the sword on the ground I put my hands in front of me. William looked at me as if I grown that second head again, a look I had become accustomed to.

"Attack." I told him.

He shrugged and came at me again, swinging the sword he held up from the ground. Judging the sweeping motion upwards and the speed he went at, I brought a leg up until the top of my foot hit his hands knocking the sword lose. Moving towards him, I brought my fist upwards into his stomach as he glared at me. Backing up, I gave him space to pick up his sword, moving around him in a circle until I picked my own up, breaking it on my thigh into two pieces I assumed another position which had a look of confusion coming across his face. Again, sideways in the direction he was, I dropped the sticks to my side and dropped my head towards the ground, watching him out of the corner of my eye as he circled like a bird coming in for its prey. As he went around behind me I watched his energy, felt it moving, the changes it made as he made a decision to come at me. Just as he was swinging his sword upwards I brought first one stick against his side, turning as I did and brought the other into the arm opposite, as his sword dropped down, missing me again. I moved away from him, letting him come at me again. Dropping the sticks as he did, grabbing hold of the wrist that the sword was in and twisting until his arm was behind his back, causing an arch to form in his back as he strained against the pain it was inflicting on him. As I pushed forward he went to his knees. Letting go of him I grabbed the sword he had dropped and swung it, bringing it to rest against his neck.

"This is how one must finish. Remove the head." I said loud enough for the boys to hear. "Not the heart, as some beings will fight even if their heart has been penetrated by a blade. If you remove the head, they cannot think, they cannot fight."

"Or so you think..." William whispered, turning on his knees and grabbing my legs as he slammed me into the ground. Holding me there he laughed finally, "where did you learn to fight?"

"Where I come from, I am not just female, I also am a bodyguard." I smiled at him as his face took on an expression of shock. "I also trained the prince to fight as he did not know how."

"Again, again!" The little one jumped on Williams back.

"No, not today. My bones are tired and beaten." William leaned back, holding onto the little boy as he stood up with him on his back. Reaching his hand down to help me up, as I stood he turned to the rest of the boys. Who looked to be in a deal of shock and horror, mixed with the smiles they tried to keep from their faces. "Turns out our Lady knows how to fight. Might be best not to anger her if you see her, and stay out of her way if she is fighting with someone. We're done for the day, you can go get some food. I will see you later for riding lessons."

The boys nodded as they stood up, looking from William to me, skirt still tied up on my thighs. The little one jumped off William's back and ran off with the other boys. "Bye!" He yelled back at me and waved. I waved back at him.

"Might want to drop your skirt down a bit." William looked at me, "I think they saw more than they thought they would."

"Huh?" I looked down, not seeing a thing wrong with the way my skirt was.

"They are boys, they do not need the image of my Lady with her skirt up to her waist any longer. Untie it and let it down where it was meant to be." He gave me one of them sideways smiles and raised his brows as he looked at me.

"Oh... of course." I fumbled with the knot and let the skirt drop. "Forgot."

"Of course you did." He shrugged, picking up the wooden weapons we had been using, "so you truthfully were a bodyguard?"

"Yes. Is that surprising?" I watched him shake his head, indecision in his posture.

He walked to the opening of the stables, dropping the weapons in the room they had come from and coming back out. "I have never seen a woman fight, much less like you did."

"Not my fault." I shrugged. Not really caring as to the why he had not seen them do such, I had basically figured out that women were kept inside, either cooking or laying on their backs, or both.

"You fight as if your weapon is part of your body, it moves with you..." He looked at me, wanting to know why but not sure he wanted to ask the question.

"The weapon is an extension of my body. I drop it in battle, I die." I looked at him, not at all bothered by the fact that he did not understand me. "My body is a weapon, is as sharp as any sword you have."

"That is the other problem, none here fight other than with weapon. Why do you?" He started walking, hands clasped behind his back.

"Because it is just as efficient to render an opponent incapable of fighting with my hands, or legs, as with a blade. Works just as well, and sometimes that is all one has to do it with." I looked at him walking next to me, "would do you good to learn to use your body as a weapon. And not leave yourself open to attacks by raising both arms into the air with your sword. Leaves your whole chest and stomach open." I slapped the back of my hand against his middle, between his stomach and chest, just where the ribs came together.

He only nodded, ignoring the way I had struck him. We walked until we came around to where the entrance of the barracks were. Stopping there, he turned and looked at me, "you may not want to fight as such with men walking around. With anyone really. They may not be as open to it as I am, and the boys will be speaking of how you handed my rump to me for some time to come. I will convince them I let you do such so they do not spread it like a wild fire about the castle and town."

"Why?" I didn't understand what everyone's problem was.

"Because women do not act as you do here. Would be safer for you if you pretended to be like everyone else, fit in as much as you can." He watched me, seemingly waiting for an explosion, when it did not come he continued, "women, and men, who do not abide by the general ideas around here are quickly banished, or worse, killed. Is the same with most towns I know."

"I got it." I grew agitated at the idea, "I would do better to stand around staring at a wall, or cooking, which by the way I cannot do, or laying flat of my back while some man uses my body for his own."

He looked almost ready to fall over, the expression of sheer shock on his face, mouth slightly open and eyes bulging. Straightening himself as he coughed, "and might want to watch your tongue as well." He pretended to cough again, "people, women especially, do not normally say things like you do."

"You mean there are only two things to come from my mouth? Yes Sir and no Sir?" I almost laughed at him, "I will not be so blatant with my words, but I will not yes Sir no Sir anyone."

"As you see fit, but remember, I warned you... you may not get a warm welcome with it." He shrugged and went inside the barracks, leaving me standing in the street.

I returned to the building I occupied and grabbed the clean dress I had and piece of fruit, intending on finding that river again and bathing not only myself but the dress that was now covered in dust and muck.

Chapter Thirteen

I was just finishing up with my bath when I sensed someone behind me. Turning in the water I saw William, leaning against one of the tree's, watching me.

"You know, you should not really bathe out in the open like this," he stated when I turned around.

"I had to get the muck off." I shook my head, "water is chilly but works for removing the stench from a body."

"We have area's inside where you can bathe, you do not have to strip down outside." He thought he needed to tell me.

"I did not know that, but this worked just as well." I began walking out of the water, not caring if he stood there or not.

"But..." he turned his back to me, "inside there is no chance of someone coming along and seeing you."

"Do you really think I have much to fear?" I laughed as I pulled the dress over my head.

"By the way you fight, no. But still is not proper to go around bathing naked in a stream where others can see."

"Should have told me sooner... tie me up?" I walked over to him, turning my back to him.

He glanced over his shoulder before turning around, lacing the dress up. "You know now. Next time you wish to bathe, let me know and I will haul tub to your building, fill it with water."

"Or I could not tell you and come here as I did before." I teased.

"You will not." He crossed his arms over his chest when he finished with the tie. "You want to come to the riding lessons?"

"Might as well so I can watch you fall from your horse." I turned around, smiling.

"I do not fall from horses." He nodded towards the dress I had washed and the shoes I left sitting by it, "going to bring them or leave them?"

"Bring them." I shrugged, walking over and picking them up. "I will put the shoes back on before I leave the hard dirt of the road for that mud you have inside the walls."

"Be a smart idea, would have to wash your feet again if you did not." He turned, walking back towards town.

"What have you been doing?" I asked, referring to the time that he had been away from me after I beat him.

"Resting." He glanced at me beside him. "I normally do not rise as early as you woke me, and I go to bed late in the night. Needed some time to close my eyes before I gathered the boys again."

"Do they have parents?" I asked, wondering if they did not and that is why they all stayed in the stables.

"They have parents. Most of them, their fathers are knights, parents live not far away. A couple of them, their parents live outside the walls."

"Do they ever see them?"

"Yes, they spend a week inside the walls and a week at their home." He looked at me, "we do not take boys and stick them in a room to be left without their families."

"Could have fooled me." I smiled knowing they did not do that, but not being able to resist the urge to be a thorn in his side.

"I know you think we are cruel and mean hearted, no feelings." He laughed, "but, is how things work, cannot be changed."

"Can be changed but will not be changed is more like it." I elbowed him in the arm.

"Are you always so rough?" He looked me over. "Hitting people, running your mouth, being mean?"

I sighed, "most of the time, yes."

"And you think I am mean..." He chuckled, shaking his head.

"Benefits of being me." I smiled as I elbowed him again.

"One of these days, someone may strike you back." He grew serious.

"Would hope so." I laughed, "do not want to think the entire world has gone soft enough to let me push them around."

"And what would you do if they did strike back?" He was curious.

"Strike them again, harder... knock them to the ground and stand on them." I joked, only being half honest as I would not stand on them, I would probably harm them more.

Shaking his head he came to a stop as we came to the entrance in the wall. Waiting for me to put my shoes on before he continued any conversation. "Do you want to ride?"

"Might as well." I looked up at him, "may show you a thing or two of that while I am at it too."

"I will saddle a horse for you then, after I saddle my horse. Meet me in the pen directly outside of the stables." He started walking again, towards the stables where again the boys were lined up against the side of it on the inside. "Ready are we?" He looked at them.

"Yes Sir." The eldest answered.

"Well get to your mounts and ready them for riding." I heard him tell them as I was walking out of the other side of the building.

Chapter Fourteen

Perching myself on the wooden plank that made the top rail of the pen, I waited a while until the boys started coming out, leading horses behind them. William had a rope in each hand, a horse on either side of him. As the boys went through the open gate they began getting on the horses, the little one was lifted up by one of the older boys. William came to stand in front of me, looking up at me sitting there like a bird on the fence.

"You going to ride the fence or the horse?" He handed a rope to me. "Your going to ride my horse today, this one is young, not well trained, do not want you falling off."

"Are you not worried of falling off?" I made fun of him.

"Just get on your horse and mind your mouth." He shook his head, leading the horse into the pen. As he moved his foot into the stirrup the horse started moving around, as if trying to avoid letting a rider on it. After a good amount of time he finally managed to get the horse to stand still long enough to let him on it, once on it, the horse wanted to go, tried to run to the other end as he manhandled it to a stop, head pulled around to his leg.

"He needs riding lessons, don't you think horse?" I looked at horse who was nuzzling my leg. Hopping down from the fence, I moved around to horses side, petting his neck before hauling myself up into the saddle. Mimicking what the others had done, I put my feet into the stirrups, horse did the rest by going into the pen and standing in the middle of it.

"Going to sit around and watch or take part?" William got the horse he rode to move somewhat in my direction, it was too interested in the activities going on around it to listen completely.

"Thought I may watch..." I smiled at him, "wait for the horse to dump you."

"I told you, I do not fall from horses." He glared at me, but I sensed something else.

"Might want to hang on then." My smile grew as I sensed the horses energy building.

"What are..." He got cut off as the horse jumped straight into the air, off all four feet at the same time, before landing on it's feet again and tearing around the pen while William seemed to try and turn it into the fence.

The boys ignored him, riding in a group, the first coordinated action I had seem them make. First at a walk with the horses around the pen, two by two, turning together, moving the horses sideways together before picking up that bumpy gate again. Around the entire enclosure again, and then picking the pace up again.

William's horse still jumping one direction and then the other, running straight for a few paces and turning sharp enough to tilt him over one side or the other. Finally coming next to me and stopping abruptly, William went over the horses head and landed on his backside not five paces in front of the horse and the horse immediately sat down on it's rump.

"Told you to hang on." I felt the urge to laugh coming to

the surface.

"That you did." William grumbled as he stood up, brushing himself off and coming back to the horse who stood back up when William was in front of him.

"Want me to show you how tis done?" I laughed at the look on his face.

"If you want to land on the ground as well." He handed the rope up to me, hanging onto his horse as I got off.

"He just does not understand does he?" I petted the horse that had dumped him. Moving around to it's side and unhooking the tie around it's middle, dumping the saddle off it's other side. "He needs to go slow, not choke you..." I continued to talk to it soothingly, petting it and rubbing it's back while William shook his head watching me and the boys. The horse rubbed it's forehead against my arm as I led it towards the side of the pen.

"That tis enough for this day boys," William called out, "go ahead and take the horses to their pens, be sure to brush them down when you put them up." The boys rode out of the gate and into the stables.

"*I am going to get on,*" I thought to the horse as I crawled up the side of the fence. "*You will feel me sitting on your back, if your good we will take that rope of your head.*" I petted it while standing on one of the rails, leaning towards it with my hands on it's back. It looked back at me for a moment, chewing the metal around in it's mouth. Moving slightly I balanced my weight between one of my feet and my hands as I moved my other leg over it's back, "*easy and slow...*" I kept encouraging it. Lowering my weight slowly onto it's back it stood there, I could feel the energy coming from the horse and could sense it was uneasy.

Moving my hands up and down it's neck, *"tis okay, I will not harm you."* Leaning over, I laid my head next to his neck, closing my eyes as I reached my hands up towards it's ears, sliding the rope over it's head and letting it drop on the ground. "Shh..." I whispered to him, letting my hands slide back down his neck to his chest. Sitting back up, I squeezed my legs into his side, *"walk,"* I thought to him as he took a step, *"that tis it, no need to run."*

Walking the horse over to William, it stopped directly in front of him and his horse. He shook his head and watched me sitting there, on the horse that had dumped him. "How did you do it?" He asked finally, tilting his head slightly to look at the horse.

"I talked to him." I answered, running my hands over his neck again.

"Talked to him?"

"Mentally, thought what I wanted to say, touched him gently..." I smiled, "removed that obstruction from choking him."

"Hm..." he nodded, looking down at the saddle laying on the ground, along with the blanket that had been on the horse.

"He is young, uneasy. You need go slow with him, not choke him and jump on him." I scratched between his ears.

"Like you jumped me?" William laughed.

"You are not young, I need not go slow with you." I smiled, sliding off the side of the horse.

"But..." William got off his horse, petting the one I had been on between the eyes, "I am well trained. Jumping on me does not send me running in any direction."

"No, you just fall from your bed." I laughed at him, turning around as the horse followed with his nose to my back. All the way into the stables the horse kept his nose against my back, stopping inside, the horse stopped behind me, *"go to your pen,"* I thought to him, as he moved his head from behind my back and walked off, putting himself into a pen a few sections down from where I was.

"Might want to stop your tricks before they burn you at the stake." William stood behind me with his horse next to him.

"Hm?" I looked back at him.

"You speak to animals, they listen to you. You fight better than my men. And you seem to have an ability to do anything you want." He listed off some of the things I had done, "they may burn you at the stake thinking you a witch."

"They can try..." I smiled at him, walking off towards the stall the horse had gone in, closing the gate and rubbing his forehead.

William put his horse up, brushed him down slightly and came to stand next to me. "I have training with my men to do, you are welcome to come with if you want."

"I think I will see to other things." I turned around.

"Stay out of trouble." William gave me a look, almost as if he knew I was up to something.

"I do not start it, I only finish it." I smiled.

"That is the point." He sighed, "just try not to do anything in front of people." He turned and walked off, back out the stables towards the pen we had just been in. Leaving me standing there to do whatever came to my mind.

Chapter Fifteen

Walking back to the building I stayed in I knew exactly what I was going to do. Stepping inside, I removed my shoes, took the cloth that lay on my bed off along with the head rest, or pillow as William referred to it. Folding the cloth and setting it down on the bed, I laid the pillow on top of it. Turning, I emptied the vegetation from the basket they were in and placed the cloth and pillow on the bottom, before replacing the vegetation inside of it. Setting the basket near the doorway, I pulled my shoes back on and picked it up, leaving the building and the enclosure of the wall. I looked at the man sitting against the wall and walked out of town, once I reached the river, I went to my right and found a clearing nestled between some trees. Setting the basket down, I spent most of the afternoon sun finding stones and wood laying around that I could use and moving them back to the clearing where I left the basket.

  Once everything was sorted out, I stood in the center of the four piles of stone, raising my hands and envisioning four walls with a break in the front wall going up. Opening my eyes, I had exactly what I had pictured, four standing walls and a doorway in one side that faced the river. Moving towards the wood pile, I laid wood across the top of the building, picturing the wood becoming one with the stone walls as I went. Laying the flatter branches and wood I had collected together, I waved my hand over it, melting the wood together into one piece. Lifting it, I held it over the doorway that I left, running my hand down one side of it, connecting it to the stone so that it would swing open and shut. Carrying the basket inside, I set it into a corner of the building along with other pieces of wood and dry leaves, leaving enough for a fire for a few days.

Leaving the building I had erected, the sun was beginning it's descent, but I still had time to finish what I set out to do. Walking back to town, I soon found the old man, much in the same place as he had been when I left the walls. Walking over to him, he looked me over, not asking for anything, not moving away, just watching me until I came to stand in front of him.

"Come with me?" I reached a hand out towards him.

"Where?" He asked, not trusting me completely.

"Your home." I smiled at him, pulling him to his feet.

"My home?" He looked confused.

"I have built a building for you, there is food inside, along with a blanket and pillow. Enough wood for a fire for the next few days also."

He gave me a look of surprise, not being able to speak. Walking beside me, I helped him move along as he had a limp, one of his legs had gone bad. Reaching the building just as the sun was setting over the hills in the west, he stopped, almost choking on his breath as he looked at the building.

"I am sorry it is so far from town, but I did not have a choice." I told him.

Looking at me again, his eyes started watering. I could feel the happiness coming off of him, he wasn't sad, he was beyond happy. "Thank you." He hugged me quickly before pulling away, as if he realized he had touched me.

"Your welcome." I told him, "want to go in? Start a fire before the sun sets completely?" He nodded and started limping towards the building, pulling the door open he stepped inside, looking around as I followed. "Sit down, I will start your fire. The blanket and pillow are under the vegetables and fruit in the basket."

He moved over to the back side of the building, lowering himself, one leg straight as he did so. Turning towards the area that I had cleared for the fire, I moved dry leaves on to it, small sticks. Striking the fire stone I had picked up against each other, sparks flew, catching the dry leaves and starting the flames that ignited the sticks. Laying a few pieces of larger wood on top, I watched it until I was sure the flames would start burning them also. Turning as I stood, I picked up the basket and turned towards the old man, taking a few steps and setting the basket down beside him.

"Why?" He asked, wanting to know why I had built him a home and brought him food.

"Because no one deserves to live with nothing." I smiled at him. "What happened to your leg?" I looked his right leg over, he kept it straight no matter where he sat.

"When I was younger..." He coughed, "it was kicked by horse, broke bone, never healed correctly."

"May I?" I put my hands over his leg, watching him. He looked at me, just as confused as before, but he nodded his head. "This will not hurt." I smiled, closing my eyes as I moved my hands, barely inches above his thigh, downwards over his knee. Seeing his bones in my mind as I went, I saw the problem, the knee had been shattered, never set and it healed wrong. Stopping my hands from moving, I held them over his knee, healing what I could of the pain and muscles around the bone. I could see my hands in my mind, there was white light around them, almost causing them to glow as I looked through my minds eye. Opening my eyes, his mouth was almost hanging open as he looked towards where I had my hands. "Feel better?" I asked, drawing his attention to my face.

"There is... there is no pain!" He looked up at me. "What did you do?"

"I healed your knee, where it had been shattered... as much as I can. It may never heal completely, but the pain should stay gone." I realized what I had done, something in front of a person, "you cannot tell anyone. They would kill me if they knew."

"I will not! Never! If it means I die with the secret of what you have done, I will not say t'was you." He was overjoyed, moving his leg, bending it at the knee. "You are..." He started to say something, but was cut off as the door of the building flew open.

Standing, I turned around, ready to kill anyone that stepped through the door. But instead of robbers, I saw William standing there, looking from me to the old man. He didn't know what was going on, he was confused and could not find words to ask any questions.

"I am almost ready to go back." I told him, watching him look around the building and look it over as if he was looking for something.

"Where did the building come from?" He asked, stepping inside of it.

"I built it." I answered him. The old man standing up behind me.

"Why?" He looked from me to the old man again.

"He needed a place to live." I glanced back at the old man, he seemed afraid to step out from behind me.

"How?" He glared at me.

"Magic..." I told him the truth in terms he would understand, but he took it as a joke, smiling at me.

"When did you build it?" He ran his hand along the stone of the wall.

"Today... after I left the riding lesson."

"Hm..." He shook his head. "Here I thought you in trouble."

"Why would I be in trouble?" I folded my arms over my chest.

"When I did not find you in your room, I asked around, one of the boys saw you leave the walls. I asked people out there if they had seen you, they said you took the old man from the wall and left town." He looked at the old man, "did not take a smart man to pick out the stone building where it did not belong."

"She did nothing wrong..." The old man started, moving out from behind me.

"Tis okay, I know him." I smiled at the old man, knowing he was used to the knights, thinking them a rough bunch.

"She is all wrong." He looked at me, his eyes laughing as the light of the fire danced around the room. "But she did not do wrong by giving you home. We will make sure food is brought out, wood collected when you need it."

"On your life you best." I watched him, making sure he was telling the truth.

"He has my word. If you take him under your care, must mean something, and by doing so he is now under my care." William shrugged, turning towards the opening again.

"He is not like the others." The old man whispered.

"He has been stuck in my company..." I smiled at him.

"Thank you." He said again, moving about the room without a limp in his step anymore.

"If you need anything, find me, or William." I looked at him, moving towards the doorway.

Chapter Sixteen

Stepping out of the doorway I almost walked into William, who was standing there, arms crossed over his chest, looking at me. "What?" I asked, closing the door.

"You could have told me you were building a home, I would have had people help you." He turned and began walking off.

"I did not need any help." I followed behind him.

"So you mean to tell me, you built the entire building on your own? No masons, no carpenters, no nails from what I could see in this faint light?" He stopped, looking down at me again.

"Exactly." I smiled, walking past him.

"How? When?" He began walking again.

"I answered those questions already." I was tired, needed to rest, and did not feel like sitting through an interrogation.

"Aye, you did. But I do not believe it."

"Believe what you want." My head was beginning to hurt, the more aggravated I got the worse the ache got.

"You could just tell me the truth." He was walking next to

me again, instead of behind me.

"You would not understand it, nor believe it, if I did. There is no point." I walked faster, leaving him walking behind me again.

Making my way back to town and towards the wall where the opening was. He didn't try to make any more conversation with me, he just followed, a few steps behind. Walking to my building, he was still behind me as I stepped inside, removed my shoes and went towards my bed. Dropping my entire body down on it before the body hit the floor.

"Are you alright?" He had taken his boots off and come to stand over me.

"I told you, I was tired." I snapped at him.

"You are just going to go to sleep, no explanation for what you have done?" His hands seemed to gravitate to his hips.

"Correct." I rolled over, putting my back to him and closing my eyes.

I listened to him grumble, the footsteps as he moved back towards the door, putting his boots back on and leaving, almost slamming the door behind him as he went. Finally silence was around me and my body wasted no time in falling asleep.

Chapter Seventeen

I awoke to find the sun higher up in the sky than normal, I had slept through the night and well into the morning. Rolling over in the bed, I saw William, sitting against the wall, watching and waiting. Was no surprise, I normally did not sleep til this time of morning.

"You going to sit there all day?" I asked.

"If you stay in bed all day, then yes." He looked worried again.

"I just needed to rest." I stood up from the bed, "what is it we do today?"

"I have to go into town. Thought you may like to come along?" He pushed himself to his feet, moving towards his boots by the door.

"What are you doing in town?" I wanted to know before I agreed to do anything.

"Picking an item up for a friend, who has found himself otherwise occupied with the Queen today."

"I'll come." I agreed now that I knew it would be a short trip, I wanted some time to think to myself today. Moving over to where he stood, I pulled my shoes on as he opened the door and stepped out. "So what is this friend doing with the Queen?"

"Escorting her. She is out in town today, more than likely shopping for some new materials or crafts." He shrugged, closing the door behind me.

"Hm..." I stretched the body and yawned.

Walking out of the wall and to our left, down the main street of the town where the markets were, I noticed the group of people down the street a ways. "Tis the Queen and her guards she is using, she draws attention when she comes down here."

"She doing any good while she is here?" I glanced up at him.

"If by good you mean an appearance, yes. If you mean by your standards, no." He gave me one of the looks that said he did not want me opening my mouth, "I am going to step inside here, mind yourself."

"Of course." I smiled, knowing it would annoy him.

Watching him shake his head as he walked inside of the building, I assumed it was a store of some kind, sold something. I turned my attention back towards the hoard of people, picking out a few of the knights I had seen walking around. I didn't know them by name and had no reason to, yet in any case. I am sure if I stayed here long enough, decided to stay that is, I would learn who they were, who they all were. The people began to break up a little bit as the group came this direction, I got my first look at the Queen then.

She was an older woman, her hair had begun to turn gray. A bigger woman too, slightly large around for her height, but that could be considered healthy next to other people I had seen whose skin appeared to hang off their bones. She wore an awful looking dress, not awful in it's appearance, but awful in how it seemed to fit. Pulling the belly in, it seemed to be a cinch like that you would find on the saddles they used with the horses. The skirt poked out the sides like some trees drape down from the top. And the top, seemed almost as tight as the cinch she wore. Pushing her breasts up to her chin practically, the shoulders of the dress on the very edge of her shoulders.

A crown of golden thorns on her head, her hair neatly pulled back. Looking back towards the doorway William had gone in, I wondered when he'd be back, I'd rather avoid meeting her if she made her way this direction, she had an energy of arrogance. And not the kind of arrogance that could be funny, but one that needed to be beat from her.

Looking back over I almost exploded from the inside out, pushing a child away from her and kicking at one of the animals near by. It was uncalled for and convinced me she needed to have that air of nobility beat from her body. Without any thought on the matter I walked towards her, the knights knew me from inside the walls and did not even try to stop me as I walked straight at her. She lifted her hand and swung it towards another animal, grabbing her wrist before it struck the animal I glared at her.

"What do you think you are doing!?" She hollered as if I was breaking her arm. Which I could if she wanted something to cry about.

"You do not strike animals, or children the way I have seen you do. It is not right." I tried to keep my voice as calm and level as I could.

"You do not tell me what to do, you..." She began to use an

insulting tone, so I twisted the wrist in my grip to silence her.

"Show respect for those around you or I will see you on the ground." I glared at her as the knights nearby began moving closer, finally realizing I was not going to let her go. "Where I come from, nobility does not give you the right to act like a..."

"Just what do you think you are doing?" William cut me off from the insult I was going to throw in her face. "Let go of her!"

"Excuse me?" I turned around towards him, still hanging onto her wrist and forcing her to move forward as I turned. "She is lucky all I have done is hold her!"

"I said let her go." William stopped a few steps away from me, staring at me.

Glaring back at him, I let go of the woman's wrist, with enough energy behind it to knock her off balance, pushing her backwards. "Fine." Turning back to face the woman pretending to be a Queen, "you should be thankful your arm is still attached to your body."

"How dare you speak to me like that!" She almost seemed on the verge of tears.

"Lucky you be that speaking is all I am doing you wretched woman!" I turned slightly as I felt William's energy coming towards me.

Chapter Eighteen

Bending slightly as he wrapped an arm around my backside, lifting me into the air, positioning me over his shoulder he began walking off.

"What..." I slapped the palm of my hand as hard as I could against his back. "What you think you are doing!? Put me down! I was not finished!" I began pounding my fists against his back, "I say, put me down! This instant! I demand you unhand me you foul smelling..."

"As you wish my Lady." He said as he dumped me over his shoulder into a pile of straw.

"Just who do you think..." I began again, trying to stand and straighten the dress I wore.

Turning, he took two steps away from me to the doorway of the shed. "She was overcome, she gives her apologies."

Glancing up I noticed the wretched woman I was speaking to moments ago, "I am not!" Stumbling out of the straw pile I went for the door. William glanced at me momentarily before stepping out of the doorway and pulling the door shut behind him. Reaching for the handle I pulled, trying to open the door as my blood was beginning to boil to the surface, "you open this door up right now! Or so help me!" I screamed over the mumbled voices on the other side of the door. Pounding my fist against the hard wood of the splintering door, giving up I kicked it one last time just for good measure and turned away, my hands balled into fists at my side as I felt the body begin to heat up with anger.

"Just what you think you were doing?" Slipping back inside and shutting the door behind him, he stood in front of it to make sure I didn't leave. "Do you have any idea of whom you were lashing your tongue at?" Turning around I crossed my arms over my chest and glared at him, attempting not to attack him even though every fiber of my being wanted to strangle him where he stood. He did not but glare back at me, shifting his position as he held a hand to his forehead, sighing as he closed his eyes. "Lady Nesenty, you will need give her your apologies before this day is done."

"I will not!" I screamed.

"You will or she will see you strung from the rafters!" He took a step towards me, coming barely inches from me and staring down at me.

"So hang me!" I pushed him away from me. "I will not apologize for lashing her! She deserved worse!"

"She is the Queen!" He stepped towards me again, hands poised on his hips as he grew angrier.

"I do not give a..." I began screaming at him again, biting my tongue before I broke into another language in front of him. "I do not care if she is made of gold, she deserved to have her hand cut from her body!"

"You will not act as such again." He stepped towards me again, the man was trying to back me down with his size.

"If you take one more step..." I began the threat.

"You will what?" He stepped again, and again he was inches from me staring down at me with a crooked smirk on his face. His eyes were laughing at me even if he kept it from his mouth.

I couldn't hold it in anymore, rising to the surface was all of the pent up energy I had been blocking out every time he scolded me. My hands went to his chest and pushed, followed by a serge of energy throwing him backwards. "I will..." I began the threat again as he burst into laughter.

"You'll throw me around? You will strike me?" He righted his posture and stood straight again, "Lady, I do not know where you come from, but will be a long time before you push me anywhere!"

Taking a swing at him while he stood there, so smug in his position, I forgot my training and did not anticipate his reaction time as he grabbed a hold of my wrist, effectively stopping the movement. "Let go of me!" I yelled.

"So you can strike me? I think not." He glared at me.

I relaxed my face as I took a deep breath, "No, so I may do this." I tried to smile at him as I moved closer to him, standing on my tiptoes and moving my hands to his shoulders. He looked down at me, not trusting but not sure on what else I could mean, I felt his body relax, and then rammed my knee into his groan. Dropping my hands from his shoulders I slapped him clean across his cheek. "Do not scold me as if I were a child!"

William grabbed my shoulders, his fingers digging into the skin and bruising the bone under the pressure of his grip. His face contorted up into a mix of pain and anger as he pushed me hard enough to knock me back into the pile of straw. "Damn you woman!" He growled out as he turned and left the room, slamming the door closed again as he left.

Chapter Nineteen

I could feel my blood boiling again, staring at the door he had slammed. The man had scolded me as if I were a child, then slammed the door, leaving me in a room with four walls slowly closing in on me. Reaching for the door I nearly ripped it off it's hinges as I swung it open, stepping from the room I found two of the stable hands trying not to look towards the room I was in and three of the other knights laughing with each other. Trying to advert their gaze from my direction, when I glared at them they turned their backs to me to continue joking with one another.

Stomping my way out of the stables, my hands balled into fists at my side, the air hit coldly. Almost a freezing sensation against my skin which was hot from anger and something else I couldn't begin to describe. Walking across the street I flung the door to my room open and entered, slamming it behind me before I threw myself onto the bed. Mentally calming myself I drifted off into sleep. Waking up some time later, I was a lot calmer than when I had entered, I could breath the cool air without freezing from the inside.

Standing up I removed my shoes and moved towards the hearth of where the fire normally was, squatted down and arranged some of the sticks and leaves that were in it, I heard the door open, sensing William behind me, I refused to look back at him even as he moved behind me until he was staring down at the top of my head. I fiddled with a piece of wood between my fingers, waiting for what I felt coming.

William felt guilt over how he had acted, and had convinced himself that he deserved what I had done. He may not have deserved it, I knew I overreacted, was much the way I was, always have been, but if he wanted to feel sorry about it, that was fine by me.

Pretending to cough as if he had to get my attention, he shifted his feet slightly before speaking, "My Lady..." He choked back another small pretend cough as he turned away from me, "...I apologize for my actions earlier. You were correct in your assumption that I treated you as a child," he turned back around and I sensed the change in his energy, "but you must understand you can not speak to the Queen the way you did. Tis not the way someone speaks to her, or her husband, or their children!"

I turned on my heels, still squatting down, looking up towards him, "if she acts like she is above her people she needs brought to her knees. And if her family acts as such as well, I will bring them to their knees along with her."

He threw his hands up into the air, slowly dragging them down the front of his face as he glared at me. "But they *are* above the people!"

"No," I stood up, staring up towards him, "they are not. They are as flesh and bone as anyone else. They need to realize that, and instead of holding themselves above, lower themselves down from that perch they sit on!"

"Ah!" He growled at me. "Should we go for a walk?"

"Changing the subject?" I folded my arms over my chest.

"Yes... Yes I am because I cannot take any more of your tongue."

I burst out laughing, watching that same look come over his face as had come over many a persons face when they were first near me. They all had the same look of disbelief and utter confusion until they got to know me.

"What are you laughing at?" He accused me.

"Not a thing. Let us go." I grabbed my shoes and pulled them on, moving towards the door as he still stood in his place. "Are you coming?" I looked back smiling at him which only made him frown and shuffle himself out the door before me.

Chapter Twenty

Walking slowly out into the field I closed my eyes, letting the tops of the grass trail under my hands as I moved. I could hear the breeze rustling through the grass, smell the trees, hear horses insentient chewing behind me, and feel William watching me.

"May I help you?" I turned, finally having enough of the feeling of his eyes. Horse was the first to respond, he looked up from his chewing and watched me for a moment before nudging his friend.

William looked at horse a moment before catching on, looking back at me, "what?"

"I said can I help you?"

"Oh, ah... no." He slumped down, sitting next to horses head and fiddling with the rope in his hand.

"Do you ever just sit out here, listen to the world around you?" I couldn't help but ask, he seemed so... strange. He slept, he ate, he rode, he bowed down before some people and towered over others.

"What do you mean?" He looked up at me, playing with the petals on a flower before horse took it from him.

Going over to them I sat down in front of him, petting horse on the nose briefly before he went back to eating on the grass, trying to think of how to put it. "I mean... do you ever listen to the birds, hear the earth under your feet breath, listen to the trees as they whisper?"

"Yes, the birds warn when someone approaches, the trees make noise as riders go through them." He looked confusingly at me.

"Not like that. I mean, listen to the animals speak to you, talk to you like I am. Listen to the trees tell the stories they hold. Place your head against the earth and hear her breathe, feel her breath." Sighing I doubted he would ever understand what I was saying.

"Sometimes... I guess. When nothing else makes noise around me." He shrugged, watching me sit and pick at my fingers. "Do you?"

"All the time. They no longer speak to me though, not like they used to."

"Like they used to?"

"Another time, another place. Long ago." I chuckled, "tis nonsense now, things have changed too much."

"What do you mean changed?" He asked as he leaned over, laying on his side and letting go of the rope which was attached to horse.

He looked genuinely interested, but I had to be careful, he would not believe half of my life if I told it to him. "I mean... where I come from, we do not eat our brothers, they are our family, they talk to us, in their own way. You can feel the earth breath as you lay against her, closing your eyes you can hear her." I laid down in the grass, putting my head to the ground, listening, trying to feel her and showing him what I meant. "The trees, the grass... they whisper to you, tell you of the tales they know." Opening my eyes I saw William had done what I had, laying his head to the ground, ear against the Earth, closing his eyes, palms feeling the dirt under the grass, breathing in slowly.

Horse walked over to me, breaking William's attempt to follow directions. "Horse, leave her be."

"He is fine, likes me he does." I smiled, I may not have been able to communicate with him like I should have, but I could pick up on his feelings.

"You do have a way with... him, you seem to have gotten under his skin." He closed his eyes momentarily, shaking his head.

"*Lay down.*" I thought to horse as I watched William begin fidgeting once again, this time with a blade of grass between his fingers. Horse lowered himself slowly next to me, continuing to munch on the abundance of grass around.

"How do you do that?" William looked at me, squeezing his brows together.

"Do what?" I petted horse along his neck.

"Get him to do the things you do? Be clam and not run?"

"I talk to him."

"So do I."

"You talk at him, not to him. Tis a difference." I smiled,

laying my head back against horses neck and closing my eyes. "Try thinking your words to him, instead of speaking at him." When William failed to respond, I peeked by slightly opening my eyes, watching him sit there, watch me as if I was going to sprout wings and fly off. "Tell me of why you wear clanking metal and live with a group of men."

A smile came across his face, in that sideways way it did. "What do you want to know?"

"All, tell me everything." I closed my eyes again, feeling horse breath behind me.

"Well..." He sighed, "I grew up in the town outside of the castle walls. My father was a knight, my mother sewed clothes for people. I was always on hand for the mucking of dung out of horse stables. One day, after my father had been gone for many months, the troop returned and carried three bodies with them. One was my fathers, my mother slowly cried herself to death. Another knight took me under him, raised me with his own son. When we were, maybe 10 years, he began training us, with swords, knives, grooming of horses. By 15 we were... studying under him for knightly positions, learning the oaths, receiving blessings from the priest. At 16 we began training with the new troupe, some of them you know today. By 17 we were knighted by our King, we swore our lives to him."

"What happened to the boy you studied with? Have I met him?" I broke in on his story.

"No, you have not, he passed some years ago. A sickness took him."

"Go on." I encouraged.

Chuckling he continued, "there is not much else. Here I am."

"Well why have you not found a mate, why do you live with men?"

"Tis a wife..." He glanced at me, "and I have not found one because... I had not found one I could stand. Most of the women in the town are..." He sighed, trying to find the right words, "...too tame, like most of the horses in the stable. They have no head on them, no ability to act of their own."

"Are you not worried of leaving an heir?"

"Ha... an heir to what? My sword? My horse?" He laughed, laying back in the grass.

"Maybe. Unless you have a hidden stash of gold somewhere." Most humans were worried about leaving their possessions to someone, offspring or nephews and nieces.

"No, no gold besides what is in my pouch." He watched the clouds in the sky now. "What of you?"

"What of me?" I sat up, letting horse get back up before he rolled on me.

"No family, no husband..." He chuckled, "or mate as you call people?"

"Do not feel the need to always be scolding a man for not using his brain." I admitted one of the many reasons.

"Men do not require scolding." He sat up slightly, leaning on his arm.

"Oh but they do." I smiled at him. "They require it by the day, sometimes twice a day."

Shaking his head he looked down, then over to horse who perked up at the riders coming our direction. "I wonder what they did this time." William said to himself.

"Told you men require scolding." I smiled again as he looked at me before getting up.

Standing, he crossed his arms and assumed that position he did. It was a mix of two different stances, one of pride and command, one of annoyance at being in command. His shoulders straight, arms over his chest, leaning most of his weight onto one foot or the other, head cocked to the side slightly, his back held rigid. It was kind of like his sideways smile, it was neither a smile nor a growl, but a mix of the two, and it was always to left side more so than the right. If it weren't for the energy coming off him I doubt I would be able to read when he was annoyed or found something funny, he closed off most things and if you had to tell what he was thinking by his body language and facial expressions you wouldn't be able to.

Horse didn't seem at all bothered by the approach, he watched them, but he didn't move from his position of eating. He was very tame at times, and other times he danced around as if there was a fire somewhere. Always throwing his head around and nickering when he saw either William or I coming down the hall in the stables. He came when called, most of the time. William could whistle until the sun went down and horse only came when he felt like it, but if I called to him mentally he'd come 9 times out of 10.

"Your presence is required at the hall." The rider in front said as his horse came to a stop.

"Why?" William asked, wanting to know the details before he committed himself one way or the other.

"Our King wants all to be present when the Lord over the sea arrives." The rider glanced at me before returning his stare to William, "marrying his son off he is, found a daughter to one of the Lords he finds suitable."

"Matching pairs again is he." William muttered under his breathe as he turned around. "I will be along shortly." He waved his hand over his shoulder signaling the men he was done with the conversation.

"Aye Sir." The rider in front turned his horse, followed by the others, and rode back off in the direction they had come from.

Walking over he reached his hand down towards me, standing there, one hand extended while the other held the rope to horse. I debated with myself over whether or not to take it, but I could feel him growing impatient.

"We must go." He stated as he pulled me up.

"I got that." I informed him that I was indeed able to hear.

"I will drop you off and then after I make my presence known I will return." He slid his foot into the stirrup and mounted the horse, reaching down again. Horse sensed William's annoyance and began dancing in place, his feet moving this way and that, stomping, chewing at the grass and bit he had in his mouth. "Lady, are you coming?" William prodded when I patted horse on his nose, stilling him.

"Yes." I looked up at him.

"Well?" He moved his hand as if I had gone blind and could not see it when it was still.

Shaking my head I took hold of his hand and let him pull me up behind him. Turning horse and riding at a good pace, quick but not fast, leisurely but not slow either. We made town in a matter of minutes, looking around as horse slowed to a walk it seemed the entire town was readying for the arrival of this *Lord* as they had called him. Cleaning the streets up and packing things away, moving cattle out of the middle of the street, children being washed and bathed. As horse walked through the entry of the wall the men were doing much the same, cleaning their armor or sharpening their swords, others were bathing themselves outside.

I caught sight of one down to his... pants if you could call them that as he washed his hairy body and laughed while joking with another. I turned my head from the sight and closed my eyes, laying the side of my face against Williams back. "What tis it?" He turned his head around and his torso slightly to look at me.

"Just protecting my mind." I offered, which was true. I was protecting it from the mental image I did not want embedded on my eyelids.

"Wait here, I will return." William stopped at the building that he had converted for me to stay in.

As he helped me down I felt the urge to be a nuisance rise, I took hold of the skirt of the dress between my finger tips and thumbs, lowering my upper body down slightly, at the same time I made the most feminine voice I could muster and said, "as you say."

William looked down at me as horse began smelling the building over, "you need work on that curtsey." He shook his head and turned horse to go.

I stood outside watching him as he took horse to the stables, dismounting and handing the rope to a young boy near by, issuing him orders before turning and stalking off to the barracks. He stripped of the hooded cloak he wore as he went, throwing it through the door onto his bed as he stepped up into the building. Bending and removing the boots he wore and setting them near the entrance before going any further inside.

He was a strange man, always stalking about, t'was no wonder people never knew if he was about to scold them or glare at them, he seemed so off of everything, as if he held everyone at a distance. But I knew better, when you made him laugh, either by doing something or saying something funny, or by annoying him beyond his ropes end. He had a sense of humor, it was just getting to it that most found trouble with, and it was purely lack of trying on their part.

Turning I went inside of the building. It had held old cloth that needed mending, along with straw which was used to soak up the wetness outside. William had carried all of the cloth out and moved it into the barracks, leaving the straw to be moved by some young boys he had ordered to do such. He had also manhandled a wooden frame into the building, throwing a straw and grass filled bed onto it, along with blankets and a head rest. He had converted it to a living area for me, insuring I was not out of reach should I find I needed help with something, "*because you have no family no husband*" he had put it, as if I could not care for myself.

Chapter Twenty-one

Going into my room I removed my shoes, setting them by the door, and sat on the bed. Watching the walls around me. The noise outside was growing as people moved about in every direction, the reasoning these people used made no sense. '*So what if some Lord was bringing a bride to the King's son. The marriage would most likely take more effort than they were worth.*' I thought to myself.

Some time passed, I remained sitting on the bed, closing my eyes and trying to block out the sound coming from outside. The door flew open as William stepped in, dressed in a white shirt and dark brown pants, his faced shaved clean and something draped over his right arm.

"Put this on..." He looked me over, "...I'll bring a bucket of clean water so you can clean up a bit." He tossed the cloth on the bed next to me and left the building, shutting the door behind him.

I looked the cloth over, it was a jade color with thread around the hems of it that had a gold color to it. The neck of the dress did not seem to be a neck at all, it looked more as if it hung like a robe. Moving it slightly there was something underneath it, another garment that felt stiff and had strings dangling from one side of it. I was not sure what it was, nor where it went, so I didn't bother trying to figure it out. Standing up I loosened the tie behind my neck and wiggled until the lace of the dress loosened enough to slip it down over my shoulders and off my arms. '*Why am I listening to him?*' I asked myself as I dropped the dress down to my hips where it rested in place.

Hearing the door open again I half turned and looked behind me as William stepped in with a bucket of water, looking towards the floor and setting it down he closed the door before looking up. Shock washed over his face and his jaw almost fell from his mouth, "my God woman!"

"What?" I asked accusingly.

"Could you not wait until I had left you? Instead you begin before I even give you privacy!" He turned himself around, putting his back to me.

"Do not try and tell me it is something you have not seen before because I would not believe it." I shook my head. I felt his energy change, one of embarrassment coming off him now instead of the shock which had been there a moment before.

"Ah... just wash up and put the clothes on I brought." He coughed, trying to cover his embarrassment over as he moved his foot to nudge the bucket beside him.

Picking up a cloth from the bed I moved towards where he stood, squatting down and dipping the cloth into the water and wiping my face with it, following up with my hands and arms. I washed any skin not covered by cloth before standing back up. He still stood in his position, arms crossed over his chest, eyes closed, his back towards where my bed was. I couldn't resist the urge bubbling to the surface to use his own chivalry against him, I nudged his arm with my hand, pushing hard enough to cause loss of balance in him.

"Damnit!" He grumbled as he caught himself with a hand

on the frame of the door. "Are you dressed yet?"

"Can't figure out where this stiff cloth goes." I picked it up, looking it over. It had arm holes and seemed to lace up the back. "Does it go over the dress?" I looked back over my shoulder just as he looked over his.

"Are you jesting me?" He looked confused again.

"No, I honestly do not know what this is for." I turned a bit more.

"No no, stop turning." He closed his eyes. "Turn your back to me and I'll help you." I held my mouth tightly closed, attempting to stifle the laughter beginning to come to the surface. "Have you turned around?" He asked after a few moments.

"Yes." I turned quickly so that I was not lying. Looking over my shoulder I saw him peek first before opening his eyes and sighing in relief.

He moved towards me, stopping just a step behind me. "Hand it to me." He reached around as I held it to the side for him. "Put your arms up above your head." I did as he instructed as he held the garment over me and put it up and over me, sliding my arms into the holes in the sides, down over my head until it rested on my shoulders, covering my stomach and back, barely covering my chest. "Now... um... adjust yourself in it."

"What do you mean?" I saw no reason to adjust anything, it was on.

"Dear Lord..." He mumbled under his breath. "Your... your breasts, adjust them inside so they do not get flattened and hurt."

"Why would they hurt?" I asked as I reached inside, lifting them up slightly.

"Because I am going to close the corset. Tie it up and it will tighten against you and if the... if your not adjusted inside it will hurt."

I finished and removed my hands from inside the garment, "What are you tal..." I was cut off as he yanked on the strings dangling in the back. "What are you doing?" I asked as the *corset,* as he had called it, was tightened.

"I am closing you up, hold still and stop moving or we will have to begin again." He warned me as I tried to turn around. "Take a deep breath." I took a deep breath and he yanked harder on the strings that were laced through the back, it was a good thing I had done so because the air was cinched out of me as he yanked a second time higher up, holding it tight as he tied it off. "All done." I felt his hands leave their position near my neck.

Looking over my shoulder I could barely move as I saw him turn his back to me again. "Why am I wearing this? I cannot move, I cannot breath!"

He chuckled, "because if you did not the dress would not fit correctly."

"But if I cannot breathe I cannot remain in a standing position!" I informed him as I tried to suck air into my lungs which felt as if they had been collapsed. "The fit of the dress will not matter much if I am on the ground!"

"You'll get used to it." I heard the smile in his voice, "many women say that it is painful to be beautiful." He was now trying to stop the laughter from coming to the surface.

"I don't want to be beautiful... especially when tis painful to do!" It was actually getting easier to breathe, I now understood what horse felt like with the rope around his middle holding the saddle on.

"Do you know how the dress goes on?" He was trying hard not to laugh at me, but it was seeping through non-the-less.

"It goes on like the one around my hips?" I figured I should ask because it might not.

"Yes." He sounded relieved, "but it t'will fit a bit different. When you have it on let me know, I'll tie the back up."

Bending over I slid the dress down from my hips to the floor and stepped out of it as I reached for the one laying on the bed. Holding onto what I assumed was the shoulders I stepped into it and pulled it upwards, sliding my arms into the holes at the top. It had short sleeves on it instead of long ones, these only came to my elbows if I had the dress positioned correctly. "Is it on right?"

He looked over his shoulder before turning around, "needs moved up a bit," he stepped towards me again, "here." He reached for my shoulders and pulled the cloth up until it covered just the edge of the corset underneath, turning me he began lacing the string through the eyelets in the back of the dress. From the small of my back all the way up to the middle of my shoulder blades, and then he moved back down my back and pulled the strings tighter, closing the dress up until he was again at my shoulder blades. Tying it off at the top, he turned me back around to face him, "*now* it is on correctly. You should have laced it before you got into it, would have made it simpler to tie up if you were doing it on your own."

I looked down, it was like two rocks protruding out of the

dress. "I am falling out of it!" I glared at him.

"Actually," he chuckled, "that is how it is meant to fit. That is why you wear the corset under it."

"I'm not wearing this, take it off!" I ordered.

"Why?" He tilted his head.

"Because it is uncomfortable, the other dress is fine."

"No, it is not. Your going with me to this event, I am not leaving you alone with unknown people wondering around."

"I can wear the other one." I argued with him.

"No you can't." He was growing irritated. "You will wear this one because you are not a servant."

"I said take it off." I repeated my earlier statement.

"A few hours time will not kill you!"

"It might! I might choke to death from it!"

"You will not! Women wears these all the time, you can wear it for a few hours!" He glared back at me.

Standing there we didn't move, just glared at each other. I wanted to punch him again, I wanted the dress off but I feared I could not turn myself enough to handle disrobing it. "Jaka-shi!" I spit out at him, insulting him even though he wouldn't understand what I had said.

"Suck it up!" He yelled at me, not at all caring if he

understood what I said or not, he knew I had meant to insult him. "Hold your breath if you must but you will wear this for a few hours."

He came towards me, turning my back to him again as he grabbed a hold of my hair, running his fingers through it and pulling it upwards. "What are you doing?!" I tried to turn and move away from him, he just held onto the hair and grabbed my shoulder.

"Hold still. I am pulling your hair out of your face."

"Why? It was fine the way it was!"

"Be silent and hand me the ribbon laying on your bed."

I looked down, I hadn't seen it there before, it must have been under everything else. *'Saving the worst for last!'* I thought to myself as I reached down and handed it to him.

Tying it into my hair to form a tail near the backside of my head he let go, stepping back, "there, all beautiful." He smiled at me.

"You wear the dress next time!" I grumbled as I headed for the door.

"Your shoes?" He was laughing as I tried to stomp towards the door, unsuccessfully as it was hard to move in any coordinated order with this torture device strapped to me.

"What?" I turned around.

"Your shoes, might want to put them on before you step out." He picked up the shoes he had set next to the bucket of water, again something different that I had not noticed before.

"Are these going to inflict pain as well?" I glared at him.

"No, but they are clean and they match the dress."

"Fine!" I grabbed them out of his hands and pulled them on, again turning back towards the door.

"Hold your skirt up when you walk or you'll trip over it."

I began grumbling in my own language as I yanked the skirt up from the floor until it was near my shins, "get the door!"

He could not contain the hysterical laughter any longer, it burst out of him as he opened the door and I charged my way out of it. Still grumbling as I trudged along. I heard the door close behind me as he followed me, his laughter trialing me. "Towards the castle, try to look like a lady instead of a wild bore charging a hunting party." His laughter burst into another round as he tried to catch up with me.

Chapter Twenty-two

By the time we reached the inner wall I had stopped *charging*, but the glare had yet to leave my face and William was still smiling as he now walked next to me. "Will you refrain from lashing your tongue at people?" He nudged my arm,

"I will not speak at all..." I took a deep breath to emphasize the reason, "...I cannot breath well enough to speak!"

"So the corset has a positive result." His smile grew bigger as I glared at him. "Stop here." He took hold of my arm and turned me to face him just before we were about to enter a building. "Try to look pleasant, no glaring at people. If you can't smile, don't make any facial expression. Stay next to me, do not wonder off, do not speak unless spoken to and it requires you to open thy mouth. Do not scold anyone. If you don't know them, you don't need to know them. Straighten your back and stand up with your chin up." He lifted my chin slightly so I was looking straight ahead.

"How could I get any straighter!" I accused him again of the torture device cinched around me.

"Be silent. Woman do not talk as you do and you will frighten people if you speak like this and get yourself killed." He gave me a warning look, "we will go in and immediately go to the King and his wife, their son, and the Lord and his wife who have brought their daughter, try to curtsey even if you fail doing so when I bow down. Do not fall if you can help it."

"You mean do not faint from the lack of air."

"Lady Nesenty, can you please try to remain out of trouble?" His pleaded with me, more so in the look he had given me than his words.

Feeling no need to respond to him I turned, rolling my eyes as I waited for him to resume his position next to me as if I was on a leash. As he stood next to me, he moved his left hand under my right arm, so that my hand rested on top of his. Looking down at me he raised his eyebrows, silently asking if I was ready. Again instead of answering I moved forward, almost jerking him forward with the movement, purposely trying to annoy him into backing away from me.

As we walked in some of the other Knights were already there that I knew, there were some that I did not know, and many people I did not recognize. I assumed some of them were the wives and families of the Knights, others had to be the ones who came with this Lord who had brought his poor daughter to marry the King's son, I felt bad for the girl. I had met the Prince's mother, if he was anything like her the girl would have a sorry excuse for a mate.

William basically led me to where I saw the Queen seated, with her husband to her left, and their son on the other side of the King. To their left, on a slightly lower level, sat the Lord, a woman I assumed to be his wife, and another, younger woman who almost looked like a child. William bowed his head to them and I tried my best to seem at least slightly coordinated as I bent my knees and lowered myself slightly. They nodded and William straightened up, helping me by lifting my arm slightly so I could stand. Walking off to the left, he led me off towards the far wall. I got the feeling he was making sure I didn't scold the plump little woman of a Queen again.

"Are we done now?" I leaned towards him whispering in his ear.

He smiled as he looked down, "not quite. The announcement hasn't come yet."

"What announcement?" I was beginning to grow curious of their customs, even if against my own will.

"The betrothal. Will be a week before they are married, but for now they will be escorted around to get to know each other."

"She looks kind of young to be mating." I murmured.

"She is 15 or 16 years. Is of a decent child baring age." He shrugged his shoulders.

"They expect her to have a child when she is still a child?" I looked up at him.

"To ensure the heir, yes." He looked at me as if I should have known. "Tis how it is done, marry them off young to ensure they have at least one if not many children."

"And how old is the Prince?"

"He will be 27 years within the month." He glanced up towards where the Prince was seated. "Be quiet now." He whispered back at me as the King stood up.

"My fair people, as you know my son has yet to marry. But that problem has been fixed, my Lord Richard has brought his daughter to help in this matter. They are a good match in body and soul, our priests have agreed with this and may God bless them with many children in the years to come. The wedding will be in four days time and you all are welcome to come." The King spoke, reaching his hand out for his son to stand up, along with this 'Lord Richard' and his daughter.

The man prattled on for what seemed like forever, I blocked out the scratching voice and looked over his son and the girl he was going to be married to. Neither of them seemed to mind, outwardly anyway, they seemed to be used to this kind of thing. The Prince had sleek black hair and brown eyes, a gentleness in his eyes that he most definitely did not get from his mother. He was well built, appeared to be strong, and quite tall, and had a presence that seemed powerful. The girl, soon to be his mate, was a contrast to him, blue eyes and long blond hair that twirled around her shoulders. She was a tiny girl, couldn't have been very strong, and she seemed to have a meek personality by the way she held herself.

Suddenly everyone in the room hollered, jumping slightly at the sound of them making such a fuss it vibrated through the room. It took me a moment to realize William had done the same as everyone else, I looked up at him as if he had lost all sense. Looking down at me he smiled, "now we can go..." He glanced around the room, "unless you are hungry?"

"Couldn't eat even if I was." I shrugged, it was true, I could not stuff food into my body when it was tied as tight as it was.

"Then let us go, leave as quickly as we can. If people stop us, do not speak." He warned me with a look again as he began to lead me off again.

Rolling my eyes I followed next to him. He would nod or smile at people as we made our way for the doors, not stopping to speak to anyone. I sensed he was trying to avoid people, and his energy changed when he failed to do so as a man stepped in front of us.

"Good evening." He slurred out.

"Good evening to you as well. A happy occasion it is!" William pretended to be happy, but his energy said differently, he didn't care for this man at all.

I looked him over, from his toes to his balding head. He smelled of rotten fruit and had missed a spot or two when shining that armor of his. His face was slightly wrinkled and sun worn. His head, balding towards the top. He looked awful, almost as if he were sick and dying, but I assumed it was just the consumption of the alcohol he held in his hand.

"I see you found a Lady who can stand your moods?" He looked at me, the way he looked though, made me want to reach out and choke him. There was an energy about him, about the way he looked, that seemed off, as if he was up to no good.

"Actually no." William shifted his weight around, tightening his hold on my hand as he looked at me, "she is a friend."

"Married?" The man looked at me but asked the question to William.

"No. I am seeing her home now." William was growing impatient. He didn't trust the man, anyone who could feel his energy could tell that, even those who could not feel it could tell it.

"Why does she not stay? Could be a fun night for all involved." He tried to step sideways but stumbled slightly.

"She needs her rest. Has been a long day."

"Does she have a name? Does she not speak?" He moved

his hand somewhat in my direction.

"I have a name that you may not know," I moved so I would be a position out of sight of the other people near by, grabbing his wrist and putting pressure against the nerves that ran his hand. "And I can speak, but not to you."

"Nesenty!" William whispered into my ear. "Let go of the man." Looking at him I let go of the mans wrist with a shove, he stumbled backwards slightly into another who laughed and patted him on the back.

Just that quick, momentary touch had allowed me to see more of the man than I had wished to see. I had seen what he was thinking, something he had done in a flash in my mind. I knew why William did not trust him now. The man glared at me before he was turned around and handed another jug of the rotten fruit from one of the Knights I knew who nodded at William, the feeling came off him said he had taken care of the situation and we could leave.

Chapter Twenty-three

"Who was that man?" I asked as we walked back down the street. I wanted to know who he was to William, not just what I had seen of him.

Sighing he shrugged his shoulders, "a shame to the honor of being a Knight."

"What has he done to you?"

"Hm?" He looked down at me, then as if realizing he had been asked a question, "nothing really. Just... he doesn't honor any code, and when there is a tournament he doesn't follow the rules. It is more like he is out on the battle field instead of taking part in entertainment. Among other things." His face winched up a little.

"He is not a very nice person."

"No he is not. You'd be smart to stay clear of him."

"I can handle myself." I began trying to untie the top of the dress as we neared the building I was bunking in.

"Except for when it comes to a dress." He smiled, stopping at the door, opening it and following me inside. "Hold still." He untied the top of the dress and the corset underneath. "Now wait until I leave to get undressed, and drop this plank over it. Will lock the door."

"What is going on tomorrow?" I asked, beginning to wiggle to get the dress started on it's way down so I could get the torture device off.

"Nothing of importance, there will be a tournament... jousting, sword fighting, riding... your welcome to come but only if you can keep from teaching the men how to fight properly." He chuckled, remembering how I had shown him how to fight.

"Then I will remain here, will sleep all day." I shrugged the dress down to my hips as William turned his back to me.

"Then if I should want to find you, you will be here?"

"Yes."

He nodded, stepping towards the door, "don't forget to drop the plank down over it after I close the door. Good night."

"Good night."

As he closed the door I walked over and dropped the plank down from the right side so it sat wedged between the wall and the wooden hooks that protruded out from it. Holding it in place and preventing any access from outside. Turning I shed the dress to the floor and followed suit with the corset, squatting down and starting the fire to warm the room before putting the other dress back on. Picking up the corset and dress I had been wearing I laid them across a box in the corner of the room.

Crawling into the bed and watching the ceiling as I laid there with my hands behind my head, I thought over my options, staying or leaving. If I chose to stay I would have to get used to this way of life. Would be expected to take a mate, which was not on my to do list. If I left, I would be on my own, no one around me to talk to, no one to argue with. For now, I should stay here, if only for a while longer, it was a safe spot for the time being.

Closing my eyes I blocked out my own thoughts and the sound of the wind outside. Not sleeping, but resting the body for a time as I let my mind slip out and explore my surroundings. Exiting the building I found myself in the barracks, watching William as he shuffled around the room, lighting candles here and there, stripping himself of his shirt.

He was toned, built for battle, a tan color to his skin even though most of it never saw the sun that I had seen. Not hairy like most of the men around here were. He also had numerous scars across his body, some looked to be from the blade of a sword or knife while others simply looked like he had fallen on a rock and broke the skin. As he turned around to the direction that I was watching from he looked around the room, squinting his eyes, as if he could sense someone there even though he couldn't see me.

Backing out of the room I sent my mind back to the castle, the hall we had been in. Watching the people, some staggering out of the building, arms hung around the necks of women, others carrying children in their arms with their wives next to them. A few of them wrestling around or passing jugs of wine back and forth between each other. Inside there was still light, food still on some of the tables, a few people still talking with one another. The Prince was talking to his bride while maids stood near by, overseeing that he minded his own.

Nothing was going to happen tonight, I might as well go back to my room and get some sleep before the moon rose any further in the sky. Opening my eyes I stared at the ceiling until they drifted shut, passing me on into a deep, peaceful sleep.

Chapter Twenty-four

The next morning I had kept myself busy. Gathering dry grass and branches from just outside the wall and hauling it back to the room I stayed in, some for the fire, some for weaving a basket. I had learned to weave baskets by hand on Atlantis, had done it a few times in Egypt, and found that it could be relaxing now that I was sure of how to do it. It was no longer irritating to do. It was now almost midday, the sun was high in the sky. I heard some noise outside and ignored it, figuring the men were arguing over something again. They did it often it seemed.

Hearing the commotion grow louder outside, I stepped from the building, looking around to find the source. The image of William came to mind, sensing he was in pain, glancing towards the barracks I caught sight of four men helping another inside and dropping him onto William's bunk. I heard the groan all the way across to where I was. Stepping further out I didn't realize until I set foot into the mud that I had forgotten my shoes, too late now as I made my way across the area, pushing men in armor out of my way who were trailing behind the others and standing in my way to the door.

"What?" One looked down at me, "you should not go in." He tried to step in front of me.

Turning my head to the side I looked at him, glaring a heat into his head, "move."

Medieval Times & the Knight in Shining Armor

Looking down at me he creased his forehead before stepping out of my way, allowing me to enter. The same four that had carried the body into the barracks were scrambling about the building as if they had their heads cut off. William was laying on the bed, face bound up in pain, making not a sound, squeezing his eyes shut and grinding his teeth against any outcry.

"What happened?" I asked to anyone willing to answer, looking down at him as he opened his eyes slightly to see me standing there. No one answered, the men inside were coming back over with dirty cloths that they dropped into water, scurrying about gathering needle and thread as well. A boy burst through the doorway carrying a jug, by the smell that I picked up as he went past me it smelled like rotten fruit. "*I said...* what happened?" I demanded this time which brought them to a stand still.

"Lady, you do not wish to be here. We will stitch it closed, leave now." One came towards me, trying to turn me around to leave.

"No, I will not." I glared at him, "do any of you know how to sew? How to heal? Clean a wound?"

"We treat our injuries all the time, drink some of the wine, pour some on the wound, wipe the blood away with wet cloth and sew it closed." The one trying to make me leave offered his way of doing it.

A round of coughing and gagging brought my attention back to William, now being held up in a sitting position as he spit the contents of the jug out with a cough as two of the others tried to undo his armor. Groaning in pain as they set him back down, cutting the shirt he wore underneath off of him with a knife. Seeing the wound in his lower side, bleeding profusely, something was stuck inside of it and these people were just going to sew it closed.

"Everyone out!" I yelled at the men in the room. They stood still, looking at me, shock on their face. "I will not say it again, *out.*"

I took the cloths out of the water bucket, the knife out of ones hand, the jug of wine out of the boys hand, the needle lay on the bed. Stopping next to the bed, I looked at them as they slowly left the building, standing just outside the door. Setting everything down on the bed I walked to the doorway, smiled briefly and slammed the door closed in their faces. Turning around, I walked back to where William laid, blood running out with every cough.

"You will need to hold still for a moment." I told him, watching him nod slightly in agreement.

Closing my eyes I ran my hands over his side, from where his arm met his torso, down to his hip, over his stomach. Sensing what damage was inside of him, seeing his insides as my hands moved over them. Stopping where the wound was I saw the piece of wood that had penetrated his kidney, sewing him closed would only let him die slower.

"I have to cut the wood out of you before I heal you," I looked at him, his eyes opening slightly as he nodded at me. "If I leave it in and heal it closed it will fester and kill you." I reasoned with him even though he had already given me permission.

Taking hold of the knife I went over to the fire, setting the blade into the flames and the handle on the stone to let the germs that could be on it die. Walking back over I looked over the cloths they had left, they were wet but they were still dirty. Shaking my head as I grabbed the bottom of the dress, biting into it I tore it with a jerk, taking one side of the tear in each hand I pulled, tearing it farther up and to the side, back down and ripping a piece off. Laying it onto his stomach I went back for the knife, hanging onto the handle which had grown hot sitting on the stone, the blade was red as the metal heated through.

"Hold still." I told him, kneeling down beside the bed. "You will not like it if I have to hold you down." He looked again at me, almost glaring at me, as he reached up and grabbed the edges of the wooden frame of the bed next to his head.

Turning back towards the wound I used part of the cloth from the dress and wiped away the blood I could, setting the edge of the knife against his skin I looked back up at him. Nodding towards me he squeezed his eyes shut and closed his mouth tightly. Cutting into his skin, making a cut from the top of his side to the back of it, he did not scream right away, groaning through the pain and grinding his teeth until I inserted my fingers between the sides of his skin, pulling them apart. He began screaming as I cut into his kidney slightly. Dropping the knife I inserted the thumb and forefinger of the hand that had held the knife, closing my eyes I sensed where the wood was, where it had splintered inside of him, removing it piece by piece and dropping it onto the floor beside me. Once the kidney and muscle around was clear of wood fragments I placed a hand over it, visualizing it closing, healing together cell by cell. As it healed I sensed him watching me, felt his eyes on me as the pain began to disappear from his body. Removing my hand from his insides, I let the skin and tissue around the kidney closed and placed both of my hands over his side. Again concentrating on the cells, ordering them to seal closed, seeing them in my mind as they came together. I began to feel the pain in my side, I had taken it on from him, transferred his energy to myself before I released it. The dull ache in my side would dissipate before the days end. As the wound closed completely, I took the rest of the pain out of his side as I felt him relax onto his bed.

Looking up as I opened my eyes and removed my hands

from his side, he was watching me, eyes wide and pain gone from his face. I stared back at him, my hands covered in his blood.

"You are an angel." He whispered as light came through a window, settling behind me.

Bursting into a laugh I shook my head, "far from it." Standing, I picked up the cloth that I had used to soak up the blood and wiped my hands, dropping it into the bucket of water as he sat up. Again I felt his eyes on me, watching me as if I was going to evaporate in front of him. "What?" I turned back around to face him.

"What did you do?" He asked, standing up.

"I healed you... after removing the splintered wood from your kidney." I answered honestly.

"But how?" He looked at his side, "there is no mark, no pain, no stitches..."

"Because I healed you closed." I shook my head at him, rolling my eyes as I walked over to where I had left the wood on the floor, bending and picking it up, "next time, do not embed wood into your side. I may not heal you again." I handed the wood to him and headed for the door, stopping at it, my hand on the handle of it, looking over my shoulder I saw him watching me still.

"Thank you." He mouthed at me, looking back down at the wood fragments in his hand.

Pulling on the handle I opened the door, coming face to face with the men gathered outside. Looking down at my hands, dry blood still on them in places, I made my way through the group. They did not try to stop me this time, they moved as I stepped, creating a path for me as I headed away from the barracks. Glancing back I saw some of them head inside of the building, heard muffled voices on the inside as they found William standing, uninjured. Walking back inside of the shed turned home for me, I closed the door behind me and washed the rest of the blood off my hands in the bucket of water I had, drying them on the skirt of the dress before laying down on my bed. I relaxed, watching the roof of the building, listening to the noise outside, letting my energy relax and return to a normal state.

Chapter Twenty-five

That night William found me in the bed still, I had fallen asleep. I sensed someone in the room in my sleep, slowly opening my eyes, coming awake. Seeing his legs in front of me, looking up slowly at him, he stood, watching me, arms at his side looking down. He had a clean shirt on, one that was not cut up the front of it, his sleeves rolled up, clean pants and his boots. A days hair growth shown on his face, no emotion, no thoughts on his face though.

"Did you harm yourself again?" I asked, finally unable to stand the silence in the room.

"No." He answered, sitting down next to me as I sat up on the bed.

"What then?" I asked, looking at him beside me.

"How did you do it?" He looked at me before turning his gaze downwards.

"Would you like to see?" I stood up, moving towards the open door.

"What do you mean?"

Closing the door to the room I stepped back in front of him. "Would you like to see how I did it?"

"You mean... you can show me?" He looked up at me, confusion written across his face.

"Yes, if you want to see I can show you." I nodded.

"Please." He nodded. "What do I need to do?"

"Not a thing." I told him, stepping closer to him he moved back further onto the bed slightly. "Relax, open your mind to me, t'will go faster."

"Alright..." He looked at me as if I would pounce on him.

Moving closer to him, I knelt on the bed, straddling his lap as I sat on his thighs. Moving my hands slowly to his temples so that the palms rested on his head and my fingers wrapped around the back slightly. "Close your eyes." I smiled at him as I closed mine, concentrating on the flow of my mind, feeling his mind. I moved, not physically but in my mind, until it melded with his, I began thinking of what I had seen, how I had discovered him injured. Feeling him tense under me as I transferred my memories to him. Showing him what I had seen, from the moment I stepped from my building to when I had dug inside of his kidney for the wood, to the visualization I had, had while sealing his side shut. He saw himself through my eyes, he saw what I had done through my mind.

He jumped back slightly, his eyes coming open as his head come out of my hands. I dropped my hands to my legs, opening my eyes and watching him. Watching the expressions change from fear, to curiosity, to confusion as they washed over his face.

"What..." he took a deep breath, "what was that?"

"Was my memories." I told him, bending my head to the

side and watching for a panicked reaction.

"How?"

"I connected... my mind to yours, transferred what I had seen to you. I could transfer feelings as well, but t'was not many feelings as you were healed, just the feeling of what you felt." Straightening my head and watching his eyes have a flash in them, he understood what I said, but at the same time he did not understand how.

"And your not..." he coughed and swallowed, "...an angel?"

"No." I laughed at him, knowing full well I was far from what he was accusing me of being.

"Can you heal anything?" Curiosity coming over him again.

"Most things yes. Some things, like the wood, I must fix physically before healing."

"Can you give me your memories, your thoughts, anytime you wish?"

"I must make a connection to you to do it, your mind is not open to me otherwise."

"Can I give you memories?" He leaned back on his arms.

"If you wish, you can, making the connection like I did."

"Do I have to sit in your lap?" He smiled.

"No..." I tried not to laugh as I explained it, "if you were to try and transfer memories to me, you would place your hands on my head as I did yours, and melt your mind into mine, thinking of a specific memory, and I would see it through your eyes as you saw it. But you must be careful to only think of one memory, otherwise I would get a flood of your memories, feelings, thoughts and see things you may not wish me to see."

"Can you show me more of yours?" He sat up, moving his hands to rest on top of mine.

"I can, but what would you wish to see?"

"Your life." He became serious. "I mean, how you came to be in that field, where you come from."

"If I showed you were I came from, you may run screaming from the building." I knew he wanted to know, but he couldn't know. "How about if I show you other places I have been?" I tried to bargain with him.

"That would work too." He smiled again, squeezing my hands as he nodded.

"You must promise not to speak of this to others." I gave him a warning glance, I did not want word getting back to those controlling this world that I had returned, I had risked it by saving him already.

"You have my word." His eyes grew soft, he was promising me that he would not speak of this to anyone, and he meant it.

"Close your eyes and relax, I will give you bits of my memories at a time." I watched him as he closed his eyes, his face and body completely relaxing. Moving my hands from under his, he left his sitting on my thighs as I moved the palms again over his temples, fingers wrapping around the back of his head into his hair.

Medieval Times & the Knight in Shining Armor

Closing my eyes I thought of Atlantis, I thought of the waterfall and the feel of the water, how soothing it had been, how peaceful. Giving him the memories and feelings from when I waded into it, of when I floating on the waters surface. I felt his energy change under me, I felt him feeling what I had felt.

Moving from that memory to one of Kie when he was drunk, as Taki and Sakie pushed him through a window, the laughter I had felt, the humor in the moment before he fell through the window. The Princes arrival as he assumed the worst in us, how we had manhandled him into his bed and all crawled in with him. I replayed the incident in my mind for William, being sure to only show him humans and times I had with them. Sakie was not human, but he was close enough he could have been deformed, he would pass for human for now as I placed another image over him in my memory, one of a more human form, blocking out the non-human form for the most part. I felt William begin to chuckle, he felt the laughter I had felt.

Again I moved from the memory to when the fire rain had come. I picture the waterfall again, the peace I had felt before the Earth shook. How the Earth had spoken to me, the animals had stilled as I moved from the water and ran for the place it had struck. I showed him the fire rain coming down, blocking out the non-humans around from the memory as I gave it to him, not allowing him to see them. Moving from the image of it striking to the image of the Prince inside of the building as it burned our skin, forcing him out from inside and the feeling of pain that I had felt. The way my skin looked as it burned from where it lay over my muscles. I felt him tense, I felt the fear in him at what had happened, I felt him feel my pain as I was moved to the healing center.

I switched the memory of it to one of losing Aree, how I had burned her body and sent her off. To one of Kie and Taki wrestling around in the barracks, the laughter on their faces. I gave him images of people laughing, feelings of myself laughing, of fun times, happy moments.

And then I gave him the last images of Atlantis I had, of watching Taki walk away with the cut down his back. Of the blood that ran from my body with the adrenaline I had felt. Of the pain I had felt before blocking it out. Of the image of the sword in my hand. Of Atlantis sinking in front of me as the salt water burned its way through my body, of the time I had drowned.

Moving the direction of the memories again before I woke up in stasis, to the time I had occupied a body in Egypt. Of the pyramids there, solid white stone shown in the sky with a brilliant gold at the top. Of the sea's water as it washed over the beaches. The lush green areas growing out of nothing but sand, the tall bushels of grass and the trees that grew a round fruit. The buildings of stone, covered in a white smooth solid outside. The pillars of the temples, the writings on the walls, the people that walked through them. I showed him a memory of one person particularly, of her laugh and smile as I told her stories of her ancestors. The feeling of the water as I found myself walking into it again, running my hands over the top of it. The way the energy of the water had spoken to me, welcomed me home again as it remembered who I was.

Moving out of the memory of Egypt, I showed him the river I had bathed in here, the way I had sensed the animals fear of me. The way the animal had run from me and left me confused at why and the anger at realizing it was not the same world. The image of him, his horse, and the three men the first time I met him. I showed him what he looked like through my eyes, my initial feelings of him, how I had connected to horse and seen horse. Moving the memory to the time we sat in the meadow, when I had ran my hands over the grass and asked if he could hear it, feel it.

How I remembered then, how the world was before and how it had spoken to me, and how now it no longer spoke, the trees no longer whispered the stories they held.

As I dropped my hands from his head, I felt the sadness rise in him, the realization that I had known the world as a great place once and now it was a broken world, one that had been destroyed. Opening my eyes I saw the tear at the side of his eye, the understanding that the world I had known was no more. He felt the sadness I felt and he understood it. Opening his eyes and looking at me as I watched him, feeling the energy in him change, from what it had been to what it would be now. He knew I was not an angel, but he knew I did not play for the other side either, he recognized me as a being of peaceful intentions. The world he knew had just changed, he had gained a new understanding of it.

"Thank you." He whispered, barely audible but I could feel the thanks he felt.

"Your welcome." I told him, resting my hands on top of his this time. Watching as he closed his eyes again, breathing deeply as he let my memories sink into his mind.

It was a few moments before he opened his eyes again, before he spoke. "I have nothing such as that to share with you." He knew his life would not be as peaceful as mine had been for a long time.

"If you do not wish to share anything, that is fine. I do not expect it." I tried to sound encouraging to whatever his decision would be.

"I want to... I want to give you something." He laughed, realizing he did not understand how to do it. "How do... how do I give you my memories?"

"Rest your hands on my head," I wrapped my hands around his, moving them up to rest the palms on my temples, "when you close your eyes, picture my face, move your mind towards me, no physical movement, but in your mind, picture yourself moving into me. Once you can feel me around you, remember something, anything that is vivid to you, as you do so it will begin to appear in my head." I removed my hands from his, closing my eyes as I saw him closing his.

At first the images were blurry, the feelings were jumbled about, the thoughts ran as if there was no tomorrow. As the thoughts began to still and the feelings stabilized the images became clearer. I saw myself through half lidded eyes as he watched me standing in the entry way of the barracks, I felt the pain burning in his body, the feeling of wishing I was not watching it happen. I heard my voice as I yelled at those inside to leave, saw the back of his eyelids and felt the uncomfortable feeling he had felt at being left alone with me as he bled out onto the bed. The images changed as he looked at me standing over him, I felt the muscles tense in my arms as he grabbed the side of the bed by his head before I began cutting into him. I felt the skin separate as a knife was dug into my side, his side, felt the watering of my eyes as I fought back the screams building in my throat. I saw myself again as I healed him closed, saw myself as he saw me. The light shining in the window, making me appear as light almost, I felt the pain subsiding and the skin no longer feeling as if it was laid open. I watched myself walk out of the building, the confusion building inside of him as he realized he was no longer injured. The men coming inside and the shock on their faces when they saw him standing, I felt the wave of nausea come over me as I stripped the blood red shirt the rest of the way off and found not a mark on the body. I heard the voices of the men all jumbled together, the whats, the whys, the hows that flowed from them as they looked over William's body. The confusion and fear he felt rise inside of him, the confusion of what had happened, who I was, what I had done to him. Lastly, I felt the fear he felt at what would happen to me, the understanding registering in him that if people knew they would kill me out of fear. He made those in the building swear not to speak of it, he told them that he owed his life to me and he wouldn't be the cause of my life being ended. They nodded, promised to him not to say anything.

Images flashed around me, glimpses of his life as he tried to change memories from one to another but in no direction. Flashes of his parents, his training, of women in a bar, of a woman laughing up at him, of someone holding a sword onto his shoulder, of the pride he felt. Of horse when they had brought in a herd of them, of the connection he felt to the animal, of the way horse had looked at him. All of a sudden the images stopped, it was as if he had fallen out of my mind.

Opening my eyes I saw him looking over my shoulder, I heard the voice behind me, "...I did not realize you were occupied." Turning my head I saw one of the men standing in the doorway, looking from me to him.

I felt the uneasiness pass through William's energy as he didn't know how to cover the situation. Concentrating on the other man's energy, I looked for what he thought was happening so I could cover for us. Finding that he thought and felt he had walked in on something intimate I almost laughed, biting my tongue so I did not give it away I moved my head down to William's shoulder, wrapping my arms around his middle. I felt him grow confused, not sure of what to do, choking back the laughter rising I whispered into his ear, "give him what he thinks is happening, he will leave... wipe the confusion from your face."

I had no sooner finished the comment and I felt his arms wrap around my back, felt his body tense as he scolded the man in the doorway, "you are embarrassing the lady. Would you leave?"

"Oh... um... of course Sir, I didn't mean to..." He coughed back a chuckle, "I will speak to you in the morn."

I heard him turn and the door close and then I burst into a fit of laughter as I sat back up, pushing William away from me. I rolled off of his lap and fell onto the bed, laughing as I laid my legs across his lap. As I looked at him my eyes began to water at the frustration and confusion that was all over his face as well as his body.

"I apologize for that." He mumbled out, watching me as his forehead got lines in it and his brows squeezed together.

Choking down the laughter bubbling around inside before I began to speak. "Tis of no concern. The man should knock before entering."

"But your..." he swallowed, looking down at the floor, "...your honor is now tarnished. He will speak of what he saw, I am sure of it."

I couldn't fight the laughter that bubbled to the surface, my eyes watered as pains in my side grew. It was a moment before I could speak through the chuckles, "this body may have the honor of which you speak, but I do not. And I do not mind."

His face looked shocked, he tried to force a smile to his face. "Did you see the memories I tried to give?"

Sitting up as the laughter finally stilled, "yes, I saw myself healing you, felt what you felt. After that it was a blur of images as they flashed in front of you, you had no control over them. Which is fine, it gave me an idea of what you had done in your life, what you had felt." His face turned red almost as he realized I must have seen other things, I fought the smile on my face, "I did not witness that which you think I did. I only caught a glimpses of one of the women. And tis nothing to be ashamed of. The images I could give you." I laughed at him as he visibly relaxed.

"You do not mind... care, that you saw those things or that he walked in on something innocent but will speak of it as not being innocent?" He looked at me for confirmation.

"I do not mind seeing that, it will be something to tease you with. And I do not care that he saw something that he thinks was something but t'was not." I smiled at him, sitting up. "Might as well stay, he assumes you will."

"But..." He tried to argue with me.

"There is a blanket you can use to sleep on the floor." I cut him off, ensuring he knew it would not happen any other way.

"As you say." He nodded, this time fighting back the laughter he felt rising.

"I do, now off my bed." I slugged him in the arm before pushing him off the edge of the bed as he stood up.

"You are a strange breed of woman." He chuckled, rubbing his arm as he reached for the blanket and threw it out onto the floor.

"And you are a strange man." I laid back on the bed. "Tis time for sleep, close your eyes and do so."

Laying down on the floor he kicked the foot of my bed, "do not order me around." He tried to assume control, but closed his eyes and fell asleep as I watched him. Shaking my head I rolled back into the bed and watched the roof until my eyes drifted shut.

Chapter Twenty-six

Rolling onto my side I looked over the edge of the bed, William was sleeping on the floor still. I watched him, waiting for him to sense it, but he did not. I used the ribbon from my hair and dangled it over his face, letting it touch his nose and cheeks softly, he stirred but did not wake. Rolling my eyes I laid back in bed and stared at the ceiling for a moment, a smile coming over my face as I thought of the perfect way to wake him up. I rolled back to my side and looked at him for a moment, watching how he was oblivious to the world around him while he slept.

Sitting up, I moved off the bed, placing a foot on either side of his hips and watching for any sign that he would be waking up. Slowly lowering myself down until I was on my knees, the sides of my thighs touching his sides as my bum sat on his stomach, not completely though as I did not want to wake him just yet. Leaning forward I put my face right in his, "Good morning." I said loud enough to cause his eyes to fly open.

Sitting up he almost slammed his head into mine and dumped me backwards. "What!?" He looked around the room, still half asleep as he noticed the weight and then me laying on his legs, laughing. "Must you jump me? There are much more decent ways to wake a man." He gave me that look of his, irritated but finding some humor in the moment.

"Yes, I must jump you to wake you." I smiled, pushing myself back into a sitting position on his legs. "If I cannot have fun, it is not worth waking you at all."

"Do you wake everyone in such a way?" He rubbed his head, pushing his hair out of his face and trying to relax the tension in his body. He woke as if a battle had begun, it would take him a few moments to calm down.

"Yes, actually. I have a habit of waking people by pouncing on them... or poking them, or standing over them until they sense me there and fall from their beds." I smiled. I had woken more people by pouncing, poking, and staring at them than I cared to count, he was just another added to that list.

"You could wake me in a more polite way." He tilted his head to the side, his eyes almost rolling with a mixture of humor and ideas.

"If you think of what I am thinking, the answer is no. I will not wake you that way." I tried to look serious, but failed miserably as the smile crawled onto my face.

"If you think, I think, of what I think you think, I would not ask that." He raised his eyebrows, watching me, "but if you are offering..."

"I am not offering and do not take it as such." I slapped the palm my hand against the side of his head and went to stand up.

Grabbing my hand he yanked me back down, "I was not finished speaking."

"Do I care to hear any more?" I yanked my hand away and punched him in the arm, smiling at the way he rubbed it afterwords.

"Tis apparent you do not!" He tried to keep the smile off his face, "but I was going to inform you that if you wish to wake me, do so gently. Push me, nudge me, yell at me, but do not pounce on me or I may take it as an offer." He was full of an energy that caused him to try and make jokes that were suggestive this morning.

"And if I made the offer, you would know it. I have not made it..." I was cut off as the door once again swung open.

"What?!" William turned his head to look at the man standing in the doorway.

"Oh!" Came from the man as he had the same notion the other had held.

I couldn't help it, the laughter came to the surface as I rested my forehead on William's shoulder, it was the second time someone had walked in and found us in much the same position and assumed the worst.

"I asked you what this is about?" William prodded the man to stop staring and start speaking.

"Ah... um... I can wait outside." Was all he said as I heard him turn and the door yanked shut behind him.

"You know what they are going to be talking about... by now I am sure that all know where I am and all have assumptions." William tried to say it seriously, but I could feel the laughter in his words, in his energy.

"I do not care." I sat back, pushing myself into a standing position. "They may wonder and speak all they want, it does not make it so."

"I should probably see what all the interruptions are about." He stood up, almost chomping at an invisible bit.

"Aye you should, this is the second time... and both found you in a submissive position." I smiled, trying to contain the laughter that wanted to flow out.

"Tis not a submissive position!" He tried to argue with me.

"Oh but it is... you, on your bum with a woman in control. Tis a submissive position no matter what is happening while in it."

"I will see you later this day. Remain out of trouble." He gave up trying to argue with me, moving towards the door and pulling his boots on.

"You as well." I told him, again trying to hold the giggling in, as he opened the door and almost walked into the man standing just outside of it.

"Do you have no mind to knock... or stand where people will be exiting..." I heard him begin scolding the man as he closed the door behind him.

Collapsing onto the bed I let it all out, I laughed until I could not longer see for the watering of my eyes and I could feel the pains rising in my sides.

Chapter Twenty-seven

I finished weaving the baskets I had started during the day, taking breaks here and there and stepping out for fresh air, or to grab something to eat. When I had finished the baskets I took them out and gave them to some of the families I knew helped with the gardening. Walking back to my room I was as wound up as a knot, I had been in the room all day and wanted to exert some energy. But I needed to go inside for a while before I did that, let the sun set a little more. I found the door open as I reached the building, stepping inside I found William sitting on the edge of the bed. A plate of food next to him and another with vegetation instead of the meat he was eating.

"Where were you?" He asked, looking up at me while I closed the door.

"Giving the baskets I made out." I shrugged and picked up the plate of vegetables.

"How much did they pay you for them?" He took a bite of food.

"Nothing... I *gave* them to the families who help with gardening. Something for them to carry their portions in."

"You did all of that work and did not get paid?" He looked me over.

"Yes." I set the plate I held aside and laid back on the bed.

"Why?" He set his plate on the floor and continued to sit there watching me.

"Because, I have no need for the coins you carry."

"Yes you do. If you ever have to exchange them for something you want."

"I have you for that." I smiled, knowing full well that it would irritate him.

"Which will only add to what they are talking about." He mumbled.

"And what are they talking about?"

He looked at me, laughter almost creeping into his eyes. "They believe I am doing one of two things."

"And those things would be?" I sat up, trying to remain serious even though everything in this world seemed to be amusing. From the way the people acted to the way they assumed things and others were shy about stating them.

"Well the first is that I am courting you, without supervision." He shook his head, "and the other is that I am bedding you and giving you gifts in exchange for your services."

"The second is more likely." I tried not to laugh as his head came up, almost as if someone had sent a shock of electricity through him.

"Why would... how would the second be a more likely

activity?" He closed his eyes, not believing he had said it out loud.

I patted him on his back, "because, I do not want a mate and courting would do you no good. But from time to time I do find that a companion for... in the sense that they are talking, can be fun." I tried not to offend his ears as he seemed to be a private person, not used to having these conversations with people, especially the female of the species.

"So you would go to bed with a man before you married one?" He almost looked offended.

"Yes." I nodded, moving off the bed and down onto the floor where the cloth was that he had slept on.

"Why?" He moved down next to me.

"Because it requires no attachment to the person." I looked at him, completely serious in my answer.

"What do you mean?" He was confused. In his time and their society they mated for life, it wasn't a question of why but just what they did.

I thought for a moment, trying to figure out a way to explain it to him that he would understand. "In your world, you chose a partner for life, tie yourself to them and grow attached to them. They can become liabilities to you, used against you. Whereas if you simply go to bed with them, form no attachment, and do not mate for life, you do not have to have the tie or attachment with them. They do not become liabilities to you."

"That's what you think of people? Liabilities?" He was growing curious.

"Yes." I nodded. "When you care for someone, they can be taken from you, used against you in battle. They become liabilities in the sense that they are now something that you have attached yourself to."

"What about friends, or people you take to bed, is there not some kind of attachment there?"

"Yes, a minimal attachment. Something you could walk away from if you had to do so. A life long attachment though is harder, it tears at your soul to walk away from them. A brief encounter, or a brief event affords only a small attachment which can be let go easier. It does not imprint itself as deeply on your soul as a life long one."

"Hm..." He thought over what I had said, sitting there deeply in though. It was just then that I had realized he had already started the fire.

I was growing accustomed to having him around and taking no notice of the differences in the room that he had made while I was out. It was a frightening thing, off my guard when for so long I was always on guard to the slightest change. I was becoming too comfortable.

Chapter Twenty-eight

Sitting there as the sun completed set, the fire burned creating sparks of light to my right, warming the room. He sat there, fiddling with the edge of the cloth laid on the floor.

"Want to see something?" I asked to break the silence.

"Hm..." He looked up from the end of the cloth at me, no longer surprised when I offered to show him something.

"Watch my hand." Raising my right hand I closed my eyes, watching with my mind as the energy began to move around, the flames of the fire coming to life, burning higher with a stronger heat to them. I imagined the flames turning blue as they burned higher in the room, running my hand over the top of them they were burning cold. I reached with my other hand, taking his and smiled as I felt him tense. Moving his hand towards mine that I was moving out of the flames I held his a few inches from mine, opening my eyes slowly and watching the flames burn between our hands. Moving my right hand up a little he followed, the flames turning into sparks of energy between them, as I moved my hand down he moved his, closing his eyes and feeling the energy dance between them.

Sending my energy from my hand into his, he chuckled, "what is that?" He kept his eyes closed, smiling.

"Me." I watched his reaction, opening his eyes he looked at

our hands. "Our energy, dancing, touching... the flames of the fire were just to give you a visual of something that you cannot see."

Moving his other hand up as he crossed his legs completely, he held it at the same level as our other hands, waiting for me to move my other hand up. When I did the energy began to dance around those hands, it felt like a warm breeze blowing in circles, anywhere we moved our hands the energy moved in swirls.

"As fun as this is..." he closed his eyes, feeling it move, "why are you showing me this?"

"Something to do." I laughed, dropping my hands back to sitting in my lap.

"I can think of other things." His head may have been bent down, looking at his hands, but he moved his eyes up to look at me.

"I am sure you can." I chuckled, shaking my head.

His head moved up to where his eyes were as he laughed, "not that."

"What?" I looked at him, confused now, if he wasn't acting like a male what was he talking about.

His expression changed from humor to worry as he stumbled to correct it, "not that I... I mean..." taking a deep breath he got himself together, "not saying I am not interested in *that* but I was thinking of going for a walk."

"Always the gentleman?" I raised an eyebrow at him, mocking him.

"I try." He laughed as he stood up, reaching his hand down.

Shaking my head again, I took his hand, letting him help me to my feet. "Where are we walking?"

"Anywhere, just walking." He grabbed the robe he had bought me and swung it around my shoulders. "It is cooling outside, want to stay warm." He offered as he swung his robe over his shoulders.

Opening the door he stood to the side, waiting for me to go in front of him. "You do realize I am not like most women, I do not need coddled?" I looked over my shoulder as he shut the door behind us.

"Does not mean I can't do it." Shrugging as he walked to my side.

"Should we take horse?" I asked as we began to walk off.

"He is in for the night, we will be fine."

"Of course we will, I am along." I nudged his side, moving him a step away from me.

"Of course..." He pushed me back. "Did I not warn you that you would not push me around?"

"I do not recall such." I pushed him hard enough to knock him off balance.

As he righted himself I took off running into the dark night, hearing him laugh behind me. Glancing over my shoulder I saw him move into a jog behind me. Figuring since I was the only one that could adjust my eyes to the dark, it was time to play a game.

Darting around a building and hoping to the top of a short wall I sat there and waited for him to come around the corner.

"Find me." I said loud enough for him to hear and give him an idea of what direction I was in.

"Game on." He hollered back at me as he ran towards the wall I was sitting on.

Turning and dropping off the other side of it I whistled, glancing up I saw him coming over the wall and took off running again. All through the streets of the town I'd run a ways, stop and whistle or make some kind of sound for him to be able to place me and take off again, always 10 steps ahead of him. Breaking into scattered trees towards the river, the field we had been in, I called to him again. "This way." Watching as he turned to follow I smiled to myself, running off, making sure the water splashed around me making noise for him to follow. I heard him make his way slowly through the water before I headed up the bank into the grasses.

Stopping in the middle of the field and turning to watch him come over the crest of the embankment, the moon overhead was full and shining down. He was able to pick out my shadowy figure without a problem, he didn't need to be able to adjust his eyes to see me, I was the only thing standing in the field. I stood there, pulling the cloak around me and waiting until he came close to me, not but two steps away.

"Finally." He nodded at me, making a point he was glad I finally stopped.

"Could not have you breaking your neck in the dark." I smiled at him even though he wouldn't see it.

"And not worried of yourself?" He was trying to watch me,

even as hard as it was in the pitch black darkness.

"I can see in the dark." I laughed.

Watching him shake his head, "sure you can."

"I can. Hold up fingers in front of you, I will tell you how many." I dared him to challenge me.

"How many?" He asked, holding his hand close to his body as he held up two fingers.

"Two." I shrugged, turning away from him.

"How did you do that?" He stepped closer, moving his hands onto my shoulders.

"I told you." I looked over my shoulder and smiled, "I can see in the dark."

"Really?" He held onto my shoulder, making sure I didn't disappear.

"Really, I can see your brows creasing, I can see the small smile on your face." I stepped back, putting my back against his chest, whispering to him, "And... I can see the tension in your body as well as feel it."

He dropped his hands from my shoulders and stepped back, turning his head to the side and looking at me, trying to see if he could see me the way I saw him.

Chapter Twenty-nine

Laying down in the grass, I stared up at the stars. Remembering home, how I had been told I'd be on my own. At first, it was kind of strange, a little unnerving that I'd be on my own, no support or anything, but as it turned out I was enjoying it. New place, new people, a new life. Even though I was still me, the possibilities were endless. No job to watch, I didn't have to plan my days out and around someone else.... I could lead any life I wanted without people around who knew me, knew what I was. I could just be.

"...thinking about?" I heard William's voice break through my haze of thoughts.

"Hm?" I looked up at him standing over me.

"What are you thinking about?" He asked as he sat down next to me.

"Life... the difference in before and now."

"Like the memories you gave me?" He leaned down on an elbow, laying on his side.

Sighing, I tried to explain it. "Not entirely, no. More so before there were always others I knew around. Certain things were expected. I also had the support of them. When I chose to come here I was told I'd be on my own. No expectations, no support, no one who knew me."

"And do you regret coming here? Without those you know?"

"At first, maybe. I did a bit." I looked at him.

"And now?" He watched me closely.

"And now..." I took a deep breath. "Not so much. It is nice not being expected to be a certain way, be a certain person."

"It is a new start." He finished my line of thinking.

"Yes. I can be anyone... do anything."

He nodded, leaning his head against his hand. "Does that include..." he seemed almost shy, "...new friends?"

"Yes." I laughed, "you are a friend."

"Maybe more one day?" He closed his eyes, not wanting to watch my reaction.

"That is a possibility, but our customs and traditions are different." I told him. Being honest as I did find him to be a possibility, I had surely thought about it before. But a life mate? Married? Probably not, my ways were too different from his.

"How so?" He was watching me again, curious about the differences again.

"Well... your customs, you mate for life. Form family groups..."

"And where you come from you do not?" He broke in.

"No. In most cases we do not." I told him. "In our ways, we partner, sometimes have offspring, sometimes not. Normally we have more than one partner in our life time."

"I see." He said discouragingly.

"No... I do not think you do." I leaned up on an arm facing him. "I have had few partners, once or twice here or there. Not a thing long term. But this body," I pointed to myself to emphasize it, "has not had a partner."

"How can it be? You have had a partner, but your body has not?" He wanted to understand.

"My memories I shared... not all are recent. Call it reincarnated, you know what that is?" I stopped, waiting for confirmation. He nodded affirmatively. "Some of those memories were other lives, other times. This body is new, it is a new life."

"Wait," he laid back, "were you born?"

"Yes." I told him the partial truth hoping he'd be satisfied.

"In this," he pointed at my body, "...body?"

"This body was born, but no, I was not in it at that time."

"I do not understand."

"This body... the person in it, they died. I asked permission and took it after they died."

He made the sign of the cross and remained quiet for some

time before asking anything else. "Are you..." He covered his face with his hands, wiping them down his face, "...a witch?"

"Not by your worlds understanding."

"Give me a straight answer." He looked right at me, "...are you evil?"

"You have felt me, seen inside me, what do you think?"

After a brief pause he answered me "No, you are not evil."

"Still want to be more than friends?" I laughed, trying to lighten the mood.

He chuckled and rolled to look at me, "how many can say truly, they have been fiends or more, with a not evil person in someone elses body?"

"Not many..." I chuckled, "...at least who get to live in this time."

"Aye." He nodded, "best not to say such to another."

"Agreed." I laid back onto the grass, watching the moon.

"Are you cold?" He asked after a bit.

"A little." Turning my head to look at him.

"Want to head back?"

"Maybe in a bit."

"Just tell me when..." he smiled, "because unlike yourself, I cannot see in the dark. I must be escorted."

I laughed aloud at that, he was actually making a joke.

"You find me funny, or is that pity I hear in your laugh?" He gave me a look, trying to be serious.

"A bit of both. Funny you would admit your downfall."

"You are being mean." He nudged my arm with a hand.

"Not the first time I have heard that." I elbowed his hand.

"Oh?" He began running a finger over my arm.

"Aye." I nodded, "I hear it everywhere I go. Is who I am."

"I am warned." He smiled, "if those who know you say such, it must be true."

"If you ever spoke to them, you would stay far from me." I told him, it was partially true, he may run the other way at the stories they could, and would, tell him.

"Yet they stay near you?"

"They do. But they, most, have known me since being a child, they grew used to me as we grew up."

"Hm..." He closed his eyes, continuing to move the back of his fingers up and down my arm.

"You tired?" I watched him, seeing the tiredness all over his body posture.

"I could stay here." He tried to avoid my question.

"So could I. But would they not worry?"

"About who?" He chuckled.

"You."

"No, they have come to the conclusion that I bed you by the night." He laughed.

"Really?" I raised an eyebrow.

"I told you the one, Micheal, would talk."

"And you did not correct the talk?" I acted offended.

"Lady... they would have thought me lying to protect your honor I took." He smiled, "even if it did not happen, they think it did and would not believe otherwise." He leaned over so he could look at me and see I was not offended but actually trying not to laugh.

"Tis fine." I put my hand on his chest. "Is time to go back. You need to sleep for the morn."

"Agreed." He rolled away and stood up, this time not extending his hand and letting me get up on my own.

Chapter Thirty

We walked back to my room, once inside he dropped the plank down over the door and laughed as he turned around to look at me. "Making sure there are no more interruptions where you have me in a submissive position."

"Yes, we wouldn't want that now would we? Your men would soon lose respect for you." I grinned.

"They already have my Lady." He chuckled.

"Really?"

"Yes, they believe I have lost all sense."

"Care to explain?" I wanted to know exactly what sense they were talking about.

"No, not really." He grinned, "leave it at, they believe I have lost sense of my duties and oaths I took. They find it humorous."

"I find you funny no matter what sense you have or do not have." I tossed the blanket on the floor at him."

"Want me to leave?" He asked as he caught the blanket.

"No, you may stay." I had that nagging urge to tease him

building up. "But you must do something for me." I smiled, knowing it would cause his face to redden and his energy to become unnerved.

"What?" He looked at the blanket in his hands, not entirely sure he wanted to know, but he could not resist asking.

"Sleep in the bed, not on the floor." I was having a hard time containing the laughter that wanted to flood the room.

His head shot up, looking at me and then at the bed. "But... I mean... where will you sleep?"

I laughed hysterically for a few minutes, laying back on the bed and wiping the water from my eyes. Calming myself as I sat back up to look at him, the confusion not only on his face but in his entire body. "I am not giving you the bed, but you may sleep in it. I plan on sleeping right here," I patted the bed for good measure, "but you are welcome to share it."

"But..." His jaw practically fell from his face.

Standing up I walked towards him, reaching a finger out and shutting his mouth as I smiled at him. "That is the extent of my offer, you may sleep in the bed instead of on the floor. Anything else will result in you on the floor whimpering like an animal in pain."

"Yes. I would expect no less." He tried to reassure his ego in his comment to me.

"You will sleep against the wall, I need to be able to rise if any should break in."

"But... wont that make it hard to throw me onto the floor?

And should I not be the one worrying of a robber and protecting you?" He tried to assume his position as alpha male in the pack.

"No. I will protect you." I smiled at him, putting my hands behind my back, "and it will not stop me from putting you onto the floor if need be."

He had nothing left to say as he threw the blanket over his shoulder and removed his boots, moving around me as I stood in my position restraining the laughter that shown in my eyes. Crawling into the bed and moving as far up against the wall as he could, he put the blanket over himself and rested his head on his hand, elbow perched on the bed.

"Are you going to stand there all night?" He tried to fake a laugh, trying to ease his own conscious.

"I may," I walked towards the bed and dropped myself onto it, "or I may stay here." I could not stop the chuckles that rose out of me as I felt his energy change.

He was worried not only of what I had planned, but also of what his own mind was thinking. His energy told me everything I needed to know right then, he was a man with a conscious, he felt guilt, he felt honor, he felt the need to protect those around him, and he worried his own body would betray him. He worried enough for the both of us, as if I had anything to worry about. Honestly it made it fun to twist his mind and ego up because I knew exactly how he felt at any given moment when I was near to him. Oh what my friends would say now if they only knew, they would be scolding me until the sun died in the sky. Enough to bring laughter from me again as I thought about their lectures I would hear.

"What is funny?" He leaned over and looked at me.

"Just thinking." I smiled at him, rolling onto my side so I could look at him without having to twist around.

"About?"

"About the friends I have where I come from. They would be telling me not to bruise your ego and warning me to walk carefully on the path for fear of you being hurt, or worse, confused." I grinned from ear to ear, watching his expressions change.

"Maybe I should send word to them... that they must come protect me?" He tried to joke.

"Would do you no good. I never listen to them." I rolled back over so my back was to him. "Good night."

"Good night." I felt him adjust himself so he was laying down with his arms crossed over his chest, head resting on the bed, knees pulled up slightly so he fit in the bed.

Smiling to myself I closed my eyes, laughing at how he worried and how much of himself showed in the energy surrounding him. If he knew he was not a private person, he did not block his energy enough to be a private person, he would have been worried of that as well. He did all he could to block emotions and thoughts from his face and body posture, but he did nothing to block it from his energy. He didn't even realize his energy said everything about him and what was going on inside of him.

Chapter Thirty-one

Waking up I found that I had scooted back in my sleep, my back was resting against his chest. He had moved his arms from crossing his chest until one was under his head and the other was thrown over my side. The heat coming off his body warmed me against the chill in the air since the fire had died out. I laid there, wondering if he even realized the position we were in or if he, as I had, had moved into it in his sleep without realizing it.

Moving slightly, I managed to turn over to my other side so that I was facing him without waking him. Watching him sleep, again, he thought he rose early but I rose earlier than he. Always having the chance to watch him when he didn't realize someone was watching him, except on the occasion I had fallen back asleep and he had been standing over me.

Moving my arm up, I ran a finger down from his forehead over his nose, watching his facial muscles twitch under the touch. I smiled as he began to wake up as I ran my finger over his mouth and chin, feeling the stubble growing on his face. He opened his eyes slowly, almost as if he was waking up to something he always woke up to. And then it was as if it hit him between the eyes as I ran my finger down over his neck and onto his collar bone. He moved backwards, hitting his head on the wall, and pulling his arm off of me.

"I..." pausing he sat up, "...I'm sorry, I didn't mean..."

"Shush." I sat up and put my hand up. "I know. If I thought anything else you would be on the floor already."

He seemed to relax slightly and then it was as if he was hit between the eyes again as another wave of realizations struck him. A red tint began creeping over his cheeks as he moved the blanket he had over his lap and legs. "Sorry." he mumbled, looking anywhere but at me.

I started laughing so hard that I fell off the edge of the bed and hit the floor on my back. I had noticed the change in his physical body the moment I had woken up, and I knew it was the result of the way the body worked, especially first thing in the morning. Either that or it was a combination of the morning functions and a dream. Either way it was just as funny to watch his reaction. Laying on the floor laughing did me no good, as I saw him lean over the bed and look at me. The look on his face only brought another bubble of laughter to the surface. He looked and felt confused again, irritated that I was laughing at him and found the situation to be funny.

"What!?" He finally asked, almost yelling at me. As I continued to laugh he grew even more irritated with me, throwing the blanket down on top of my face to try and silence the giggling coming from me. "This is not that funny!"

"Oh but the look on your face and the way you reacted when you realized it was!" I told him between breathes. Pushing the blanket off of my face and sitting up I looked at him, now glaring at me. "I knew about it before I woke you up, but I did not expect you to panic!" I started giggling again, watching his face begin to tint once again.

"Tis your fault!" He finally smiled, trying to place the blame on me.

"How so?" I threw the blanket back at him.

"Was your idea I sleep in the bed and not on the floor! If I had slept on the floor the situation would not have happened." He almost puffed out his chest, trying to assume a position of control and knowing, crossing his arms over his chest again in that defensive posture.

"Yes it would have." I raised a brow at him, smiling, "happens every morning to most men. No matter where they sleep the night before. Tis not my fault, only blame that lays with me is that I found out about it."

He glared at me from his position on the bed while I sat on my knees on the floor. Finally a smirk forming on his face. "Maybe it does."

"Do you not have work today?" I reminded him as I noticed the light beginning to grace the Earth through the window.

"Yes I do."

"Are you going to do it or sit there?"

"I am getting to it in my own time." He uncrossed his arms realizing I was right, standing and looking down at me and shaking his head as he moved towards the door. Pulling his boots on before lifting the plank off the door. As he opened the door he glanced back at me, still perched on the floor, "speak of this to no one!" He smiled, almost laughing with his eyes as he stepped out, closing the door behind him.

I sat there until I heard the noise beginning outside from people waking to go about their day. Finally pushing myself up from the floor and sitting on the bed, looking around the room. I had no idea what I would do this day, I had too much time on my hands and not enough to keep myself busy.

Chapter Thirty-two

Pulling my shoes on and heading out of the door I decided to head to the stables, see if horse was in there or any of the others like him. Give them a treat while no one was near by.

Walking through the stables I headed for horses pen. He was already waiting at the gate for me, tossing his head around. I petted the horses as I went by, saying hello and receiving a nuzzle from them. Animals, even if too long not being heard, still understood a difference in people.

One of the other Knights that lived in the barracks was standing at the other end of the stables, leaning against the side of the opening. Horse was becoming agitated, and I could see why, I could sense the man's energy as well. He had thoughts in his head that should not be there, he would be on the ground if he acted on any of them. I glared at him as I came to stand in front of horses pen, trying to calm him down before he broke the wooden gate that kept him inside.

"Servicing all?" The man had come to stand behind me.

"Only if all entails me harming them." I rolled my eyes, not even feeling the patience to humor him.

"Sir William must have moved you in for a reason." He stepped closer to me.

I could feel his energy, not evil, but not of good intentions. "I would not do what you are thinking if I was you."

"But you are not me, and I will do what I wish." He moved closer, not protecting himself as he put a hand on my shoulder.

"You may not say I did not warn you." I smiled to myself, watching horse in front of me stomp and snort, kicking the gate in front of him.

"And you..." he began.

Reaching up I grabbed the wrist of his hand on my shoulder, pulling him forward as I put an elbow into his stomach just below his ribs. Turning I brought my elbow up, letting go of his wrist as I put it into his temple. Facing him he held his stomach, looking up at me with an angry look on his face.

"Leave." I told him, watching him straighten himself.

"Not before you do what you are here for."

"Suit yourself." I took a step towards him as he raised a hand, grabbing the wrist of it I twisted it until I felt the bones begin to crack and held it in that position as his face contorted into one of pain. "I will not tell you again."

"You wench!" He jerked his arm away, shaking it to get the numbness of nerves being cut off out of it.

Stepping towards me again he balled his fists up, now not only was his body in pain, his pride had been damaged. Horse was panicking in his stall as the others became uneasy in theirs. He took the last step between us, grabbing hold of my upper arms and glaring at me. I rolled my eyes and laughed at him before becoming serious, swinging my arms around and under his, moving them over the tops of his I brought my elbows down into the bend in his arm, braking his grip. Twisting my body as I landed a blow with my right fist into his left side, ensuring I hit hard enough to crack a rib. Turning as I stepped towards him I brought my elbow up into his face, breaking his nose as he stepped backwards.

"What?" I heard William's voice at the other end of the building.

Looking that direction gave the other one a chance to come back at me, swinging his fist towards me. I had sensed his energy moving and leaned back, dodging the swing. Moving back upright and turning, I stepped towards him, first my left fist into his liver and then my right into his ribs. I could sense William coming towards us as the other raised his hand again, moving it towards me. Grabbing hold of his wrist as I twisted my body pulling him forwards and off balance, he went over my back and landed flat on his on the ground in front of me.

"What are you doing?" William came to a stop on the other side of the man, looking both at him and me.

"The little wench!" The man groaned out.

"What happened? Tell me now." William ordered, not so much at me but including me in the question.

"I thought you had brought her here for a reason," the man got up off the ground, "was acting on it when she attacked."

"I warned you." I stepped towards him as he backed up.

"Enough!" William stepped between us. Looking at me, he

almost glared at me, warning me to stay where I was, "return to what you were doing. And you," he turned around to look at the man, "do not try such again, I did not bring her here to see to the needs of the men of the barracks, there is a woman's house in town you may visit, and do not speak of what has happened here."

The man nodded and turned, leaving the stables through the entry way I had come through, shaking his head and straightening his nose back into place as he went. William watched until he left the building before turning back to me as I petted horse on the nose.

"Must you harm my men?" He accused me, almost laughing.

"When your men have no mind to listen when I tell them to leave... yes." I looked over my shoulder at him.

"Women do not act as such here." He tried to argue his point, again, that women listened here.

"I am not from here. And if men insist on being pigs, I will break every bone inside of their body." I turned, leaning against the gate.

Shaking his head he reached over and petted horse as he hung his head over my shoulder. "You do this in public and you will be hung for your actions. Be happy he agreed not to speak of it."

"I will not be pushed around by a man." I glared at him.

"Nor should you be, but tis my fault." He sighed, dropping his head down, "I brought you here, moved you in close, and they think what they do of us. Is only a step to assume why you are here."

"Then let me set it straight to them." I stepped away, intending on going to the barracks to scold every last one of them.

"No," he grabbed my arm, shaking his head. "Would do no good, they will not try such again. Will assume I did that to him if he does not open his mouth, and if he does open it I will finish what you so elegantly began."

"Elegantly?" I almost laughed.

"Yes, very... easily began. You did not even break sweat doing such." He laughed, shaking his head and covering his eyes with his hand as it rested on his forehead.

"And I will finished it if he should try such again." I warned William, letting him know he should make it known I don't bow down to anyone.

"I will inform them tonight to leave you be." He agreed.

"Or... ?" I wanted to make sure he knew I'd hurt them if they did.

"Or they will deal with me." He looked at me. "I cannot tell them that you will harm them, to do such would mean I was admitting that you were... different. And being different here, does not allow for much freedom."

"Fine." I shrugged his hand away from me as he reached for my arm.

Stomping my way back down the stables I balled my hands into fists to keep from throwing anything as I went. The laughter behind me from him was rubbing my nerves raw. I was ready for a fight and he insisted on being calm about this. He was insufferable... downright annoying at times. Swinging my hand towards a bucket as I left the building it fell over, I didn't even touch it and it went flying because of the energy that left my hand when I swung it.

Chapter Thirty-three

I had no sooner slammed the door to the building I was in and it flew open again, fuming as I turned around William was standing there with the biggest grin I had ever seen on his face. Right in the middle of the door frame, effectively blocking my way if I wanted to leave, arms crossed over his chest, restraining the laughter and just smiling.

"What do you want?" I growled out.

His only response was that his smile grew larger. Every second that past irritated me more, I could feel the energy building up inside, almost like an explosion waiting for someone to push the button that would set it off.

Reaching behind me I grabbed the head rest laying on the bed and threw it at him, catching it he began to laugh. Stepping inside, he held the pillow in one hand and closed the door with the other. Giving me time to grab the blankets on the bed and throw them at him, he didn't try to catch them, letting them fall to the floor he shook his head. Turning my back on him I looked for something else to throw, something heavier, harder that could knock the smile off his face and the laughter out of him. The only thing left of the bed was the bed itself and the frame. There was wood near the fire, a box in the corner, and on the box was the torture device he had made me wear, '*I could make him wear it*' I thought. Deciding on the bed to begin with, I picked it up and turned, holding it between my hands it nearly touched the floor length wise up and down, covering my face, but I heard the laughter roll out of him. Tossing it forwards it bounced off of him and fell to the floor, his only reaction was to take off his boots. The man's energy was one of amusement, he found this hilarious. Balling my hands into fists to prevent any energy that might accidentally escape them I glared at him, my body was tensing up with the exertion of keeping everything inside. Turning my back on him again I began weighing the chances that the frame of the bed, *'would it bounce off of him or knock him out so I can put him in that torture device?'* Lost in my own thoughts of what would knock him out long enough for me to turn this situation around I didn't sense his approach behind me.

"Relax yourself." I heard him trying to stifle the laughter as his hands rested on my arms. Rolling my eyes out of aggravation, I closed them, taking a deep breathe and pretending to follow directions. "Good, now take some more deep breathes..."

I rammed my elbow into his side, cutting him off from any other instructions he felt the need to give. Drawing a groan from him as I am sure his rib cracked under the force. Trying to turn around to face him, back him down, he wrapped his arms around me, pinning my arms to my side as he began his laughing again as if being struck in the side was something to laugh about. Throwing my head backwards, it hit his jaw, which only caused him to tighten his arms, he was trying to make me stop by squeezing the air from my body. Moving my leg, I pushed my foot against the frame of the bed, creating the force I needed to push him backwards, slamming him into the door which caused a jarring of the wood walls around the building, and the plank which fell. Almost clipping him on the top of his head, he bent forwards and the plank hit him on the back instead.

"Would you..." He began again, tightening his arms around me again. Pulling him forwards along with me, I didn't judge the distance between us and the bed frame as I almost stumbled into it. Falling to my knees, he didn't let go but fell with me, holding my upper body up, still trying to squeeze the air out of me. He began laughing, again, "now this is interesting."

"Silence!" I yelled at him, throwing my upper body backwards, sideways, trying to wiggling out of his grip without using the pent up energy inside of me. Pound for pound he was stronger than I was, bigger, taller. Without using the natural abilities of this body he could effectively outmatch me when he had me in a grip that didn't allow for the use of my arms. Throwing my head back, as it was the only object I had that I could move in this position, I moved my torso back with it. He remembered the way I had used it as a weapon before and moved his head, pulling me back into him until his arms wrapped far enough around me to almost touch himself. "Let go!"

"When you calm down, I will let you go." He restrained his laughter while speaking to me as if I were a child.

"When you let go I'll have your head!"

"All the more reason not to let go." He chuckled, I could sense the smile on his face, the laughter radiated off him in his energy even if he kept it from escaping his body.

I began wiggling again, trying to turn my body so I could see what I was trying to headbutt, the grip almost bruised the skin, it hurt the bones inside. Maneuvering my legs out from under me I dropped to my bum, bracing my feet against the frame of the bed. I felt his grip tighten again as he knew what I was going to do. Pushing with every muscle in the legs, I threw us backwards, landing him on his back while I lay on top of him. Trying to move my hands around to his sides he let go of the hold he had me in and grabbed the wrists, pulling them backwards as he forced himself back upright. Pushing me forward he slammed me into the floor, twisting my arms around behind my back, pinning me to the floor as he moved a knee into the small of my back to help hold me down. He was breathing with the exertion of trying to hold me still, his muscles were tired from the grip they had been holding me in for so long. His energy still told me that he found the situation amusing, even though he restrained himself from laughing out loud.

"Are we done?" He sighed the question.

Weighing my predicament out, I took note of the hold he had on my arms so they crossed in the back, pinning my lower half with his knee. The side of my face was squished up against the floor, I couldn't have thrown my head any direction without risking being stuck by a sliver of wood. My options were limited, I could lie and attack once he moved off of me, or I could submit and be done, or I could be honest and tell him no.

"No!" I decided on the later of the choices, being honest, even if it harmed my being.

"You cannot move!" He began arguing with me, almost laughing at me. "This is why women do not go out alone with men! We are stronger!"

'*Oh by the stars! He is lecturing me!*' "Strength does not matter! You could be in this position and it would take no physical action on my part!" I was half tempted, even though I was calming down and the blood was no longer boiling inside of me, to teach him a lesson and throw him across the room.

His laughter rolled through the room, vibrating off of the walls as he leaned forward, keeping most of his weight on the knee that was on the floor beside me, whispering in my ear, "I could do anything I wanted to you right now and you could not stop me. Men are stronger than women. Strength does matter when they put you in a position with no defense."

"Get your hands off of me or I will harm you!" I warned him, not entirely sure I was going to toss him across the room or not, '*this is an interesting position*' I thought to myself and quickly caught it before it had a chance to fester any ideas. "Remove your hands or I will break them!"

"Really?" He said with a hint of daring in them, moving his hands he kept the grip on my wrists, forcing my arms out and upwards until my hands rested on the floor next to my head. Moving his knee from my back he set it on the other side of my body and sat on my back. "Is this better?" He laughed at me.

'*I wonder what we could do in this position... no, no... Nesenty, stop, you can control what this body does, stop letting it wonder!*' I scolded myself, closing my eyes and trying to control the thoughts coming to mind. '*It might be a good defense to play along, I might even like it, it would get him off guard... no it would get myself off guard as well... it is not an option!*' While I was debating with myself, he moved his weight down until he sat on my legs, holding my hands still against the wood flooring.

"You need to stop torturing my men..." he leaned forward again, pushing my hands upwards until he could hold both of my wrists in one of his hands, "...they would not play as nicely as I am playing. And if they got you in this position, they would not control themselves." He tried to lecture me again as he moved his free hand down to my side, touching it gently and sliding it onto my back and up until it rested on my neck. "They would strip your clothes from you," he untied the knot that held the lacing together in the back of the dress, "and do anything that came to their minds."

"The way your going to!" I accused him, half interested as I felt the heat in the body rising.

"No." He let go of me and stood up, "I am not like them."

Looking behind me he backed up, stretching his arms and neck, almost as if he was feeling the wear on the muscles. Pushing myself up, I stood, turning around and watching him. Debating with myself again, *'continue what I had been wondering, torture him, or teach him why his men posed no threat to me... the options were endless of what to do.'* I finally decided to teach him why his men would not succeed in anything they tried, even if I was on the floor and they sat on me.

"Want to find out why I am not afraid of your men, or any man?" I crossed my arms over my chest, placing most of my weight on the left foot as I titled my head slightly.

"I think we proved that they do," he no longer found the situation funny, he was serious, "just by the fact that you were on the floor under me."

"I let that happen... I was half tempted to let it go further." I almost bit my tongue off as I realized I had said it aloud.

"You what?" He looked at me, shocked and confused.

"You heard me, your ears work fine. Come out to the meadow with me and I'll show you why your men stand no chance against me." I smiled at him, "I might even let you put me in that position again."

"You have lost your mind." He shifted his weight back and forth from one foot to the other.

"If only you had known the thoughts in my head... you would know I had lost it a while ago." I smiled again, throwing a wall up between the thoughts of *'what could we do'* and *'what I am going to do.'*

"Fine, let us go then." He headed for the door, shoving his feet into his boots and moving the plank off of the door where it had fallen.

I followed behind him, laughing inside at the mess that was in the room now, we had torn it apart. Or more so I had torn it apart, he had done little to destroy the room.

Chapter Thirty-four

As we walked into the meadow he still had not changed his energy from the room. It gave away his feelings, his thoughts. I could tell the basics of what was going through his head just by the energy coming off of his being. He was curious, of what I thought I could do, of what I meant by my statement back in the room. He was irritated that he had to take the time to prove to me that men were stronger. He wanted to see what would happen out here. He had a scolding or lecturing feeling about him, aimed towards himself for what he thought he had done, or almost done, back in the room. He was a jumble of things all at once.

"Pin me." I stopped in the middle of the meadow, far enough away from any buildings and people who might see.

"What?" He looked at me as if I was out of my mind again.

"Pin me like you had me pinned in the room, here, I'll even lay down so you don't have to wrestle me to the ground." I knelt down and lowered myself until I was laying flat on my stomach. Turning my head to watch him, he stepped to my side, looking down at me and shaking his head as he closed his eyes. "Go on, sit on my legs and put my wrists in your hand."

"You need to stop teasing." He told me as he straddled my back, lowering himself down so his knees were on either side of me again and he sat on my legs. He didn't grab my wrists though, just sat there.

"This is not the position we were in, in the room... lean forwards and grab my wrists." I moved my hands above my head so that they were in the same position they had been earlier, his hand could fit around both wrists.

"This is not a good idea." He warned me, chuckling as he leaned forward and grabbed my wrists. "Your putting yourself in a position of being violated."

"You wont, and you couldn't if you wanted to." I smiled, watching him out of the corner of my eye.

"Yes, I could." He laughed, moving his free hand back and pulling the skirt of the dress up. "T'would be that easy." He stopped and moved his hand back in front of him.

"No it wouldn't." I closed my eyes and focused my energy, "brace yourself."

I felt him tense slightly, "why?"

Throwing my energy backwards, it took him with it, slamming him into the ground on his back. Standing up I walked over to where he lay, standing over him and looking down at him. The air had been knocked out of his lungs, he had not braced himself like I warned him to do. He stared up at me, disbelief radiating off him, curiosity, confusion.

"That is why your men stand no chance against me. That is why I told you the truth when I said 'I let you put me in that position.' I could have thrown you at any moment in the room, I restrained myself from doing so." I stared at him, tilting my head to the side slightly, watching him, watching for panic.

"What... what was... what did you do?" He stumbled over

the words.

"I used my energy, the energy of this body and my being to move you." I smiled, "in this case, throw you off of me. Forcing my energy backwards, it hit you and your energy like a wall."

"How?" He pushed himself up from the ground to stand in front of me and watch me.

"Every being... be it human, animal, tree... has energy around it. Sometimes it is used to tell what the person thinks, sometimes it is used to signal an illness or injury, sometimes it is used as a defense."

"You mean you can tell what people think by their energy?" He was afraid I knew what he had been thinking, that red tint washing over his cheeks again.

"No, not exactly. I do not get images of what they think, unless they share that with me. But I can get the basis of what they think, the direction of their thoughts. I could tell what you wanted to do back in the room, I could tell you still thought about it as we walked out here. I could tell you were confused, curious at my words. But I could not see what you saw in your head."

"You can do this all the time?"

"No, only when I focus on it, or am comfortable with someone."

"And... the throwing of people?" He wanted to know more, he wasn't panicking or afraid.

"Anytime I focus, yes, I can throw someone."

He began pacing around, back and forth, one arm crossed over his chest while the other rested it's elbow on it, his fingers tapping his chin. He was thinking, wondering, realizing I meant what I had said, everything I had said. Finally stopping in front of me again he looked at me, pointing a finger at me, "and your not a witch?"

"No. Nor am I an angel. I am just different." I sighed, sitting down on the grass, he sat down with me. "Not so much different, you have the same abilities, I just know how to control them."

"Can you teach me?" He was curious again.

"It would take a lot of time and you might never be able to do it. Your..." I tried to think of a way to explain it in terms he might understand. "...your spirit knows how, deep inside, but your body does not understand it. Your kind have not used it in so long it has been forgotten."

"Is this what you used when you were fighting with my man in the stables?"

"No." I shook my head, "I did not have to. He did not have me pinned, I had the use of my arms, legs, my body. He may be stronger but I know how to fight, I know how to catch someone off balance. If he had pinned me, if I had let him pin me, I would have been able to use energy against him. Nothing happens without my permission." I smiled at him.

"Well that is a comfort..." He almost grumbled.

"It should be. I do not need a sitter."

"They would kill you for using this."

"I know, which is why I don't where people can see." I took a deep breath, "your people would fear me, word would spread to those I hide from, if your people did not kill me than the others would."

"Who are the others? Where are they?" His forehead creased as he looked at me.

"They are ones who do not care for people, they may be Kings or Queens somewhere. They do not care about life, only of their own being. They control what happens in the world."

"But who are they? Surely you could stop them?"

"I have tried, I have killed some of them in battle. But it is easier to avoid them for now."

"What would you do if someone knew about you... what you can do?" He wanted to know my plan.

"I don't know. I might fight, but there is so many of your people and the others, I am outnumbered. I may just let them kill this body, I would go home if they did."

"Where is home?" He didn't understand me.

"In the stars. This body matters not, it is just something that can be used that allows me to interact with you and your kind."

He stood back up, walking circles as he thought. He had to move when he thought, to sit still was against his nature. His mind was thinking everything over and thinking about it all. Laying back in the grass I put my hands under my head and closed my eyes, resting while he thought everything over. Who knew how long it would take him, and he seemed content with the silence and wearing a path into the grass.

Chapter Thirty-five

I must have dozed off because when he finally spoke, it seemed hazy. "...just let them kill you?"

"Hm?" I opened my eyes and sat up.

"I said, you would just let them kill you?" He stared at me.

"Yes. I am not here to kill your kind. And that is what would happened if I fought them, they would die, and the others would learn about me and they would hunt me down until I was dead." I shrugged, dying wasn't that unfamiliar, I had done it twice already, and I always had my own body to return to.

"So if people found out about you, you would let them kill you, and I am supposed to do nothing?" He was distraught with the idea.

"Yes. You do nothing. I let them kill me."

"Why?" He dropped himself onto the ground, sitting in front of me.

"Because if you tried anything, I would have to protect you. Then we both would be hunted, and we would both die anyway." Human's did not seem to understand the concept of doing nothing, not that I understood it any better, but at least I had another body to go to whereas they did not have one on stand by.

"Why would you protect me if I was trying to protect you?" He had the creases in his forehead again, by the energy he got when that happened, it signaled he was thinking again.

"Because like it or not, myself liking it that is..." I smiled, "you have become a friend. I have allowed a liability in friendship. If your in danger, I must protect you because of that friendship."

"I thought you allowed no liabilities?" He joked.

"I said I do not allow life long, permanent liabilities. Friendship is temporary, it does not created the lasting attachment."

"Ha! There is a difference?" He chuckled, thinking I was joking.

"Yes, I have explained it to you before. You are a friend, I may have a small attachment to you, but it is one that is easier to let go than a life attachment, which will never happen."

The sun was beginning it's descent in the sky, we had been out here longer than I had thought. I must have really dozed off when I closed my eyes, he must have paced and thought some time. Looking around I noticed the path that was indeed worn into the tall grass.

"We should head back." He was thinking the same thing as I was.

"Yes, we should. Should eat and you need to warn your men to stay clear of me or I will have them broken in two pieces." I smiled, trying to annoy him.

"I will warn them, but I will replace the *you* with *me*, deal?"

"If you must. It would be funnier to watch their faces when they hear '*she will break you in two*' than having them believe you will break them in two. But if you want it that way, that tis fine." I shrugged and stood up, reaching down to help him up for a change.

Chapter Thirty-six

We had returned to my room, eaten some of the vegetables that were in the basket still, and he had left as I was starting the fire. Crawling into my bed as the sun went down completely, I watched the ceiling as if it would move. As my eyes began to drift shut the door opened and closed, I heard the boots being shed and the plank being dropped. I had sensed it was William and had no reason to open my eyes, I was half asleep as it was.

"Move over." He whispered as the bed gave way to his weight as he sat down.

Sliding over slightly so I was closer to the wall, "who gave you permission?" I tried to joke in that half sleepy voice.

"I did." He moved his arm under my head as he had taken over the head rest.

"Hm..." I snuggled up for the heat as he pulled the blanket over both of us. Letting myself drift off into the sleep state, I pushed my mind from the body and watched.

He laid there, eyes open, watching the ceiling in much the same way as I had done. One arm under his head while the other was wrapped around my body, his shoulder under my bodies head. He was thinking again, the old man had been right when he said that William was different. He didn't panic when I told him what I did, or showed him the things I did. He didn't have that drunk state that most of the other men around here had. In fact the only time I had seen him take a drink was when he was injured and it was poured down his throat. Returning to the body to let my mind rest along with it, he soon fell asleep as well.

Waking the next morning I found that I had assumed control of the bed, using him as a head rest as well as a body rest. One leg thrown over his middle, an arm thrown over him as well, and my head on him. While the other leg and arm were stretched out as close to the wall as they could get, touching it. The blanket was between me and him, partially on the leg that was near the wall. He was still in much the same position he had gone to sleep in. Flat on his back, arm wrapped around me and the other under his head, legs as straight as he could get them. He didn't seem to have moved at all while I tossed around and took over in my sleep.

Pushing up slightly I looked at his face, watching him. "Good morning." I tried to wake him the way I had done the morning before.

"Do you mind, I need my sleep." He hadn't been asleep, but was pretending.

I began laughing, "did you not sleep last night?"

"With all of your moving, I don't think anyone could sleep." Opening his eyes and looking at me. "It's like riding a horse sleeping with you. Must hang on and try not to fall off the bed as it shakes as you throw yourself around it."

"No one said you had to sleep with me."

"I have learned my lesson. I will sleep on the floor tonight."

"Might not be safe there either, I may roll off the bed."

"Then I will sleep in the barracks."

"Works by me." I smiled, knowing he was lying.

"I am going to go get the boys up so they can begin their chores. I might get a chance to sleep sometime today." Removing his arm from behind his head he pushed my leg from his stomach and pulled his other arm out from under me. Stretching his body to get the kinks out. "Will you not attack my men today?"

"If they leave me be, I will not harm them." I rolled onto my back.

"They will leave you be if you leave them be." Walking towards the door he pulled his boots back on, lifting the plank to the door. "You should get up, too much sleep is not good when you have not allowed others to sleep."

"I could sleep for you." I stretched out on the bed.

"Go into town, do something." He looked at me again before stepping out the door, "try to behave."

"I always behave." I turned over, turning my back to him and facing the wall.

He laughed as he shut the door behind him, leaving me alone in the room to get into trouble. After he left, I rolled back onto my back and stared at the ceiling, again, thinking over what to do today. If I could freely use the abilities of this body I could help in the town, either with basket making or seaming cloths together for clothing, but I couldn't do that. And if I could boss the men of the town around, I would have an army to train, but I could not do that either. The town had it's limits of what I could do. Most of them based on the fact that I was the female of the species, must watch what I say and do, or I may offend some poor male that needed to be taught a lesson. Must watch what I do in front of any of them, or I might scare them. The world had definitely changed, especially if everywhere you went was the same as this town.

I put my shoes on and left the building, heading into town. William had left his pouch sitting on the box in the room, so I had his coins to spend if I found the need to. Smiling to myself I shook my head, he was a strange, strange man.

I found myself at the end of the street, where the woman's house was, he had told me never to go in there, but my curiosity outweighed any warning from him. Walking inside I looked around, it had more than one level. On the first there were tables and chairs, women half dressed all through the building and a few men sitting at tables with a woman on their lap, talking to them.

"Here for work?" A woman had walked up to me on my right.

"No, just looking." I looked her over. She was a bigger woman, long brown hair, plump in the face with her chest literally half out of her dress. "Was curious what it looked like inside, my friend warned me not to come in here, but I was curious."

"I see." She looked me over. "Well, look around all you want. Upstairs there are rooms," she pointed towards the staircase, "but if a door is closed don't go in. If you decide you want to work, come to me and we will get you dressed for it." She turned and walked off.

The woman had been pleasant enough. Even the energy around her had been welcoming, not even annoyed that I was curious. She seemed nice, what she was doing here I had no idea. But the other women in here, it was not hard to figure out what they were doing. The few that sat with the men were being talked to, they laughed and joked with the men. One was leading a man up the stairs as he handed coins to her, her breasts were out of her dress as the back had been untied part of the way down. I could see her shoulder blades and part of her lower back. Her skirt was hiked up part of the way. I could guess at the services she offered, and why men paid for it. It seemed most women in this town married before they did anything with a man, was a shame, they might have had a little more fun and control if they didn't hold out like that. Most men were run by one of two things, their stomach, or their groin in this day and age, I had noticed that in the time I spent looking for a body to use. You could use food against them, or intimacy against them, both worked.

Walking up to the large table, opposite the door, it was long and made of smooth wood. The plump woman had gone behind it when she walked off after talking to me. There were shelves behind it holding jugs, and wooden cups below it. I sat down on one of the tall chairs with no back that sat in front of it.

"Want something to drink?" She smiled at me.

"What do you have?" I asked, curious if they had anything decent to drink besides the rotten fruit people seemed to drink like water in this town.

"Any kind of liqueur you could want."

"Do you have water?" I looked at her as she laughed, dipping a cup into a bucket behind the counter.

"Do not drink do you?" She set it in front of me.

"No, does not settle well with me." I told her, I had learned it wouldn't settle with me when Kie had drank of the rotten fruit, and again in Egypt when I had tasted the wine they had there.

"Takes time to get used to the taste and how it effects ones body, after that it becomes easier." She leaned on the counter.

"Do I owe you coins for this?" I asked, knowing that most things you traded coins for.

"No, water is on the house. And if you had asked for a drink instead, that would have been on the house too. I do not ask for coins from women who come in here, just the men."

She walked off a ways, a man had come in while we were talking and stopped at the other end of the long table, he ordered a drink and she made it for him, collecting coins from him as she handed the large cup over to him.

Chapter Thirty-seven

As he walked off with the cup in hand she came back over to where I sat. "What brought you in here? Besides your friend telling you not to."

"Curiosity. They told me what went on here, but I wanted to see for myself." I smiled at her, her energy hadn't changed, she was a nice woman who was just as curious about people as I was.

"Well, you could find out what goes on inside rooms by working." She laughed, "but I doubt you want to. Or I could tell you and show you around."

"Do you not have to be here in case men want drinks?" I tilted my head, watching for her reaction.

"No," she chuckled and shook her head, "the girls can handle it if I step away. Come on." She waved her hand at me as she came around the corner of the long table. As I stood up she started explaining, "down here, the men can come and drink and find company with one of the girls. Talk is all they are allowed to do down here in case someone with gentle minds walks in so they do not get offended. The bar there," she pointed to where I had been sitting, "is for drinks, no one is to go behind it unless they work here." She leaned closer, smiling, "I also keep a chunk of a log back there in case I have to strike anyone."

"Really?" I looked at her, not believing it because I had

been told women were nice here, and not outspoken and could not defend themselves.

"Really." She nodded. "When men drink, they tend to lose their common sense. Sometimes I must put it back into them before I haul them outside. Come on, we'll go upstairs, there is nothing else down here besides what you see." She walked off, waving me along towards the staircase and began talking again as we went up to the second level. "Up here is where they can get a little wilder. All of my girls keep a chunk of heavy wood in their rooms, in case they need to control the man." She laughed, "for being the protectors and providers in this world they sure are dumb sometimes. Anyway, when the man gives one of my girls, or a couple of them, coins he is entitled to a little fun. They go in a room and give him entertainment, depending on what he pays is what he gets. They close the door so people know the room is occupied." We came to the end of a hall in the second level, there were doors on one side and open in the middle so you could see down, it went all the way around the building like this. "This room here is my room, you can look inside if you want."

I stepped towards the open door and peeked in. Inside there was a big bed, it had poles on the corners of it coming up from the frame with cloth hanging down from it, a thick mattress and more colored cloth on it. Near the window there was a table and a chair, and on the other side next to the wall was another table with drawers in it. On the other side of the bed there was an opening in the wall with clothes hanging in it. A few other chairs sat in the room.

"And this room here," she drew my attention to the next room, "is where my girls can spend time together, it has various cloths for making clothes or mending older ones. Also has it's own private bar inside if they need a drink."

I peeked inside of that room, there was what looked like a bed chair, it was long like a bed but thin like a chair and had a mattress on both the bottom and the back of it. Clothes hung from the wall, a fire was burning inside of the room also. "It looks pleasant." I smiled at her as I pulled my head out.

"Should be, the girls need a break now and then." She led me down that side of the building, showing me different rooms, introducing me to a few of the girls inside a couple of the rooms. They all seemed really nice, not what I had expected when I walked in.

"Do you work here?" I finally asked as we rounded the last corner and came to the top of the steps.

"Used to. But I don't anymore. I own the building and take girls in who have no home, if they decide they want to work that is their decision." She shrugged, "my husband died years ago and I had a hard time making the taxes to the King, so I began doing this. Over the years a few of my friends began doing the same thing, eventually I had saved enough to have this building built and I began moving girls in. A few decided to do this work and it has continued."

"Are you looked down on for controlling the men this way?" I asked as we came to the bottom of the steps.

She laughed, "by the women of the town yes. But the men know their place when they come in here. They treat my girls with respect like another man, or they are struck and thrown from the building to lay on the ground outside the doors."

"William has been trying to tell me that women mind their tongues in this town and most places. He did not tell me I would find women who thought, and spoke, like I do here." I smiled, almost willing to move in here rather than continuously having to think about putting a man on his knees outside of it.

"Sir William? The Knight?" She looked at me like she knew him.

"Yes, he is the one who warned me not to come in here. Said I might find myself confronted by a man who wanted to be serviced." I chuckled, "how do you know him?"

"Well, I do not want to damage your image of him." She smiled at me and had a twinkle in her eyes.

"You could not damage the image I have of him, tell me." I sat back down on the chair without a back by the bar.

She walked behind it and handed me another cup of water and perched herself on a chair behind the bar. "Well..." she sighed, "I knew his mother years ago, and after he came of age some of the older Knights brought him in here. I treated him to a few free drinks and paid one of my girls to take him upstairs."

"You don't mean..." I laughed.

"Oh yes, I mean that." She raised her eyebrows. "He got broke in and stumbled out of here with the usual awe struck position of a fresh colt."

"Does he come here often?" I almost choked on the water I had taken a sip of, trying to contain any giggling from escaping, but she saw the laughter in my eyes.

"Not as often as he used to. He used to come here at least once a week when he was younger, but since he has gotten older he comes maybe once every few months." She pointed for me to look behind me, "that girl there, her name is Mary. She was the one who broke him in."

I looked at her, she was a pretty girl, thin like most of the women here with a chest on her that could knock someone over if she didn't pay attention where she was walking. Long tan hair and a pair of green eyes. She smiled when she saw me looking and went back to talking to the man sitting in the chair next to her.

"She normally see's to him when he comes in still. Although I have had him break in a few of my new girls before, he is a little bit more gentle with them than other men." She laughed as she dipped my cup into the bucket again and handed it back to me. Pulling a jug from a shelf she poured herself a drink. "Most men do not care to take their time with a young filly, they just go for it. But William is good to have on hand when I need one broke for working. There are few men who I trust to do it other than him."

"Do I want to know what *broke* means?" I was not exactly sure what she meant, but I was curious again, hoping she would use whatever description she saw fit to use since I obviously did not understand.

She laughed and leaned on the table, closer to me, so I followed suit and leaned closer to her, "it means when a girl has not been with a man before, she is a virgin. Breaking her in can be painful if you are not gentle about it."

"Oh!" I sat back, almost smiling, "I see."

"Good," she laughed, "because here comes my stallion for that." Pointing behind me, I looked over my shoulder as William was stomping his way over to where I sat.

"I thought I told you to stay out of here?" He came to a halt next to where I sat.

"Oh mind your mouth William." The women spoke up, chuckling as she scolded him, "she was curious and you know I let no harm come to any woman in here."

"Point is I told her to stay out." He glared at me, shaking his head.

"I might want to move in here, might be easier to beat on the men that come in." I was half tempted to make a face at him.

"That is just what they need!" He sat down on the chair next to me shaking his head, "hops please, Beth?" He looked at the woman behind the counter as she laughed and got him a cup of what didn't have the potent smell of rotten fruit, but foamed at the top. Setting it down in front of him she held her hand out. "She has the coins." He pointed towards me, smiling as he picked the cup up.

"Oh, that's right." I reached down to my lap, completely forgetting I had been hanging onto it. "How many?"

"Just give her one of the silver ones." He told me, "she doesn't realize the trading customs here." He looked back at the woman he had called Beth.

"I can tell she does not understand much of our ways." She smiled at me, "you could just give me his entire pouch and I'll see him taken care of." She laughed.

I handed her the pouch and laughed as I did so, the look on William's face as he slammed the cup down was worth it, "here. Make sure he has fun."

"You will not. I knew you should not come in here!" He grabbed it before it went from my hand to hers.

"Why? Too many others that think like I do?" I looked at him.

"Yes, yes there are. And you would be a bad influence on them." He finally smiled.

"So your warning to me was not for my own safety, but for others?" I watched him.

"Actually I thought it would be for your own safety, but I have since learned otherwise. Tis for the safety of any man that walks in that door, and the safety of the girl's sanity." He took a drink from the cup he had.

"Oh would you two just go up stairs." Beth laughed as she pushed away from the table. William almost choked on the hops he was drinking, slapping his hand down on the top of the bar as he coughed and his eyes watered. "Easy boy! It was just a suggestion." Beth patted his back as she walked off.

I smiled at him as he regained control of his breathing. "Do not listen to her." He looked at me.

"Why not? She seems to have good intentions." I turned around, leaning my back on the bar, watching her talk to the girls down here and check on the men in the chairs.

"Because if you have not figured out what she meant, then you do not belong in here." He took a long swig out of the cup, finishing it before setting it down.

"Oh, she showed me around. And told me about Mary and

the girls that need *broke* and how she uses you for that." I watched his face turn a bright shade of red. "She showed me upstairs and introduced me to a few of the girls. She even explained to me what broke meant, and told me about when you first came in here." His face turned an even brighter shade of red, if that was possible, as he stared at me, mouth almost falling open.

"She did not!" He practically yelled at me in a soft tone of voice.

"Oh, she did. Apparently you are her stallion for use with young fillies." I used the terms she had used, which only made him close his eyes and lay his head on the top of the counter.

Beth came back over with Mary in tow, and offered "she could tell you some stories."

As William sat there with his head on the table and groaned I laughed, "I would like to hear them."

"Why don't you and Mary go upstairs to that room I showed you where the girls take breaks then, I'll see that he stops his whimpering." Beth smiled at me.

I looked at William who was still moaning and groaning and shaking his head slightly as it lay on his arms on the table. "Okay!" I hopped up from the chair and patted him on the back as I followed Mary towards the stairs and up them. Glancing back down as we made the top I saw him still with his head on the bar as Beth poured more of the hops into his cup.

Chapter Thirty-eight

Mary sat down on the padded chair and patted next to her, "come sit down. Promise I do not bite." She smiled at me. As I sat down she turned slightly, pulling her legs up on the chair, "what is your name?"

"Nesenty. And yours is Mary?"

"Yes. So, what would you like to know?" She almost giggled with the idea.

"Anything you care to tell me. He will be down there whimpering like an animal in pain no matter what you tell me, so make it good." I laughed.

"Where to start, where to start... hm..." she was deep in thought, debating where to start with the stories. "I guess I'll start at the beginning." She had a huge grin on her face, "you ready?"

"Always." I laughed at the way she seemed so happy and excited, like a child almost.

"The first time he came in here, he was 16. His adoptive father, the Knight who took him in, and a few of the other older ones brought him and his adoptive brother in one night after the sun had set. We were pretty busy then as we are most nights, we work more at night than we do during the day. Anyway, they brought them in and they looked like wild animals who had been cornered and surrounded. Just that AWE kind of look on there face," she emphasized this by making the awe struck face and throwing her hands in the air, "Sir Hamlet and Jacob sat the boys down at the bar while the others began their talking with some of the women. Beth came and got me and Lillie, she's working right now or she'd be in here too, and took us over to the boys. We were younger, I was 20 at the time and Lillie was 21. We sat on the sides of the boys, them in between us as Beth started pouring them one drink after another. Anyway, skipping forward here, we took the boys up here to our rooms. I got William inside the room finally after he kept shaking his head and saying 'no, what are we doing? What's happening?' over and over again, he was always such a sweet boy, always worrying about what is going on. So I got him in and closed the door behind him and it was like that flight fear animals get in, he looked around like he was going to run right through the wall." She started laughing, throwing her head back and giggling as I started to laugh. "He calmed down after I handed him one of the cups of wine I had brought up with me and sat down on the bed. His reaction when I untied my dress and dropped it was the funniest thing I had seen in a long time. His mouth almost fell clean off his face and he stared, dropping the cup of wine I had given him and his eyes bulged out of his head almost. He didn't know the first thing about any of it, I had to teach him everything from the fact that it took both of us to strip and get under the covers, all the way to the fact that it was okay to relax and sleep afterwords."

I was laughing so hard my eyes were watering when she stopped speaking long enough to breath a little between the chuckles and the way she had been rattling on. "He still gets that look." I admitted to her, thinking of the way he had almost panicked when I was changing.

"Oh," she waved her hand at me in a dismissive way, "he is just too polite for his own good. If he would learn to relax around women he would have more fun."

"Any other stories that will make him turn red as an apple? Something I can use against him?" I laughed, trying to be serious, but at the same time I was too serious for my own good.

"I have more stories than we have time to talk about. Lets see... oh, there was the first time Beth asked him to break in one of the girls, Katie was her name, well her nickname. She was about 17, this was years after his first visit here. He had come in as he often did and I had been talking to Beth about him, and she knew Katie needed to learn the trade, she had showed interest in it and asked about it and wanted to learn it. Well Beth and I walked up to him and a few of the others that were in here, I sat on his lap and gave him a big ole kiss right on the cheek and said 'we have a favor to ask you'. He laughed and thought I was joking, and that Beth was in on it as she stood behind him. Finally he asked what we wanted, I started by telling him we had this new girl here and needed some help, he nodded. Beth filled him in on the fact that she was still just a girl and wanted to learn the trade but she didn't trust any of the men there right now to help with it. And he asked what we wanted him to do about it, stand over and watch. We both started laughing and I told him to stop being silly, we wanted him to do it. He just about ran out from under me, dropping me on the floor as he pushed the chair back and stood up, dropping the cup he had in his hand to the floor and looking at us. That wild animal on the run look he gets." She started laughing again, laying back onto the chair, my eyes watered at the image I got of him in my mind. "We finally convinced him to stand still long enough to hear us out. Took us a while to convince him it was a good idea, we introduced him to Katie and showed them up the stairs and left them alone in the room. The next day Katie filled me in... it was like his 16 year old self all over again. He was practically afraid to touch her, like he might hurt her if he did." She stopped and began laughing all over again.

"I assume he got the job done?" I was almost falling off of the chair we sat on I was laughing so hard.

"Oh he did, but only after she stripped him down to his pants and grabbed his hands and put them on her. She had to make the first move before he did anything!" Mary's eyes were watering now, she was practically choking on her words as she laughed while talking to me. "After that first one, it got easier. It didn't take us as long to talk him into it anymore and he didn't look like he was about to run anytime he was just in with a girl."

"He does this often?" I was curious.

"Not as often as it sounds. There were about five of us when he was younger who worked here, and since then a few others who didn't need to be broke have come in, and about six of them over the years that needed to be broke in have come in and worked here. So about six times, there is about fifteen of us who live and work here, besides Beth, and most of us were broken in before we started working here, but those six that came in untrained we've seen to it that he got locked in a room with them." She was wiping the tears away from her eyes as she took a few deep breaths, finally the laughter was subsiding in us both.

"Can we go now?" I heard William's voice from the door way.

Mary started laughing all over again as she laid back on the chair, William just shook his head and closed his eyes as I started giggling. "Tis not that bad!" I waved a hand at him.

"Yes, yes it is. Tis that bad and worse." He grumbled, stepping into the room. "I have no doubts of what she has been telling you, and if you have not given her some of your own stories then it is the perfect time to leave before you taint her goodness with your mean little mind." He waved a finger at me.

"But, there is so much I could tell her and teach her!" I argued, sliding off the edge of the chair as I laughed and laid my head down on it.

"No, she does not need to learn anything from you." He stepped closer, looking down at us both as we laughed until our sides hurt again.

"If she has something to teach me, I am willing to learn it!" Mary sat up looking at him, still giggling like a child.

"Arg!" He threw his hands in the air and sat in the other chair in the room.

"Is that permission?" I poked fun at the way he sat there, head in his hands.

"Beth!" He yelled, and she must not have been far off because she came around into the room not long after he called her name, "I believe I need another drink." He glanced at Mary and myself still giggling. "And bring them something too, on me."

Chapter Thirty-nine

As Beth left the room William sat back in the chair, relaxing a little, he was watching Mary and myself exchange looks and laugh. He just shook his head and rested his arms on the sides of the chair, almost like a King would sit a thrown when he was deep in thought.

"One time, he drank so much, he could barely walk..." Mary started laughing as she told me, "and by the time we got to the room, he could not think clearly enough to remove his own clothes."

"That is not how it happened!" William broke in waving his hand around, "if your going to tell her stories, tell her the entire story, not just pieces of it."

"Then you tell me." I smiled at him, watching that red tint start to creep over his face.

"I will tell you, but after you must tell us one of your stories." He looked at me, half expecting me to argue.

"Yes, you must tell us something!" Mary broke in just as Beth walked back into the room carrying a tray with a jug on it and four cups.

"Who must tell us something?" Beth inquired.

"Nesenty, William is going to correct my poor recollection of his drunk state and then she will tell us a story."

Pouring the drinks Beth smiled at me, "you have stories?"

"Yes, I do." I glanced at William who just shrugged as his cup was handed to him. Beth handed a cup to Mary and myself before taking one herself and sitting down. Smelling it, it smelled bitter, but with any luck it would taste better than it smelled. I looked at William, sipping at his, "well?"

"Yes... yes I am getting to it. Tis not everyday that you sit around with three women and tell tales of your..." he coughed, turning redder by the moment, "...your activities."

"Tis never too late to start." I smiled at Mary and Beth who started giggling watching him squirm under the realization that he was sitting in a room with three women about to speak of what he was about to talk about.

"Ha ha, you are very funny Nesenty. I'd warn you to bite your tongue, but you never heed my advice, so I will not do so." He chuckled, taking another swig of his drink and smiling, "When I was a young man I came in here more often and drank a good deal more. This little wench here," he pointed at Mary, "kept giving me drink after drink of the strongest they have, it was as if she wanted paid for allowing me to pass out in her room."

"No, t'was not like that!" Mary broke in on the story this time, giggling, "I was tired you see, I wanted an easy job for the night."

"You and everyone else." William gave her a look that almost had me laughing again. "As I was saying, she kept pouring me drinks. I don't know how many I had, ten, twenty, more? I was ready to lay on the table and sleep my night away, but she insists I come upstairs for some entertainment. So I pay her the usual nightly fee, and as I stand up, she trips me!" He glares at her, smirking that way he did.

"I did not trip you!" Mary laughed at him, "Beth tell the poor girl that I did not trip the man!"

"To be honest I was not watching the two of you!" Beth laughed, pouring herself another drink. "You may have tripped him, or..." she looked at William with a grin, "he may have tripped himself."

"I did not trip myself woman!" He sighed, laying his head back. Taking another drink as he brought his head back up, "someone tripped me, I almost fell into the table. And here is this bare bosomed little lady trying to help me stand back up straight. We make it to the staircase and I am looking at my feet, making right that they hit the steps accordingly and I do not roll back down them. Up the stairs and into her colorful room that could blind a bat!"

"My room is not that bad William, you watch your tongue!" Mary glared at him, smiling as she did so.

"Oh, yes it is. She has the sheets that cover the bed died a red color, the blanket she pulls over herself and whoever be in the room at the time dyed an awful bright pink color. Then the worst of it? She has the cloth dangling from her bed posts dyed a violet color! All accompanied by a green dyed curtain over her window." He took a huge swig of his drink and handed his glass to Beth who almost instinctively knew he was nearing empty, she poured him another and handed it back before sitting down again. "Your room my Lady, is the worst here. T'would blind a bat as I stated, it is so bright, it made me see double of all contents of the room. I swear she had four breasts that night!"

"The mouth you have on you!" Mary gasped, "my room is not that bad. I like the colors, goes well together."

"Only if you cannot see." Beth mumbled.

"On with the story." William broke them up by interjecting that he was going to finish the story if he harmed his senses or not. "We got into the room, she shuts the door and starts laying herself all over me. I'm trying to find the bed in there, something soft to rest my head on and get some decent sleep without the company of a building full of men. I keep telling her to crawl off me long enough to allow me to undress."

"Are you jesting me!?" Mary giggled, "you could not tell your shirt from your pants! Did not matter that I was paying my dues for the coins you gave me, you needed help!"

"Silence." William held his hand up, "who is telling the story? Tis not you." He laughed at the look she gave him, "I had perfect ability to find my clothes but could not get to them due to the half naked woman climbing all over me. I stumbled nearer to the bed and jammed by toes into the post of the bed, never mind where my boots went, I have not a clue as to their location or how they came off of my feet at this time. I tried to turn and fall again because of this Lady," he waved his hand at Mary, "practically falling on me. I'm laying on the bed and then she offers to help with my clothes, I am defenseless and here she is, sitting on my lap while I lay on the bed, unable to move, and she's stripping my shirt from my body!"

"And where were thy hands at this time, hm?" Mary butted in giving me a knowing look.

Biography of an Ancient by Nesenty

"T'was undoing your dress the rest of the way, but is not the point! You were attacking a defenseless man who just wanted to sleep!" He laughed, taking another drink.

"His hands began at my breasts," Mary began telling the story for him to which his face began to turn a deeper red than it already was, "roamed their way around as if he was looking for something until he found the ties here, "she pointed to the front of her dress where there were ties on her corset. "Then he begins fumbling around as if he were a young boy again. No sense of what to do or how to untie a woman's dressings!"

"I knew what I was doing. T'was taking my time I was." William got up this time and poured himself a drink, refilling Mary's and Beth's as well before sitting back down. "Hoping that the Lady would lose interest and go to sleep before I had to perform any duties to her."

"Rest it William! You were drunk and could not see straight!" Mary accused him. Then she looked at me and added, "Tis not the last time he was that drunk either!"

"Of course I was not seeing straight, have you looked at your room when you are drinking? Is like a battle field walking into the place. My hands were as she says, she removes my shirt and crawls off. Walks out of the room for a moment and I hear the door close behind her, I was almost asleep when she enters again, this time her dress is around her hips and she's pulling me upright laughing the entire time..."

"As were you if I remember right, you were laughing just as much as I was." Mary pointed a finger at him as she took a drink.

"She pulls me up and drops my pants to my ankles and

pushes me back into the bed of horrors! T'was not bad enough I was undefended and near sleep, but she pushes me into this bed that spins around ones head. The rest, you can imagine what happened because I am not repeating the actions." William shook his head, rolling his eyes as he took another drink.

"I can finish it from there because my recollection seems to be more on a correct path than one who could not find his clothing." Mary smiled at him, taking my hand and resting hers on top of it as I smiled, "the man there," she eyeballed him, "had to be led through the actions once again. He could not tell up from down, in from out. When t'was done, he passed out and rolled clean off me and almost off of the bed."

"Would have been a more decent sleep on the floor, instead I woke to the sight of the bedding." He closed his eyes as he laid his head back, staring at the ceiling of the room, refusing to look at any of us. I was laughing hard enough to bring waters to my eyes and pains to my sides. The images I had gotten from their energies were enough to send me into a fit of giggles.

Chapter Forty

"You have not drank anything?" Mary looked at me, sitting on the floor next to her legs.

"Just biding my time. I wish to be able to laugh without falling over." I smiled at her.

"Ha!" William sat forward and stared at me, "you fell from the bed the other day laughing without none to drink!"

"Yes, but that was for a reason." I looked at him, smiling as I remembered how red his face had turned.

"What happened?" Beth asked.

"He woke up in the normal way men do." I smiled, watching him as he covered his face, "and he had flung his arm over me after I had warned him my offer ended at sharing the bed."

"So the two of you?" Beth pointed at me and then at him, a question on her face.

"No!" William answered before I could. "No we have not, the body she occupies is innocent, although her mind is not. Her mind is far from innocent!"

"What does he mean?" Mary giggled and looked at me.

"I remember other lives before this. He is correct when he says this body is *innocent* but my mind is far from innocent." I smiled, taking the first sip of the drink since I was given it. It tasted just as bitter as it smelled, but I liked the way it almost sparked on my tongue and inside my mouth.

"She tortures men... endlessly." William sat back in the chair, relaxing into it.

"And you have not taught her the trade?" Beth pretended to scold him, "have I not taught you well enough to help the poor women of this town? Save them from the other men?"

"She has yet to ask me to do such, so no, I have not!" He tried to defend himself.

"Tell us a story!" Mary stopped their bickering.

"What kind of story do you want?" I took another sip, swirling the bitter liquid around in my mouth.

"Hm..." Mary was thinking about what she wanted to hear, "...something that we are all familiar with, tell us of an activity of yours." She smiled, almost as if she enjoyed sharing stories.

"Okay. Let me think." I took another sip and began to feel the effects, I was beginning to feel the tiredness setting in. "I was in another land, far from here, another time as well. I had gone there on a visit, made a few friends while I was there. And there was this one man, he had long braided, pitch black hair and brown eyes. He was older than me, had a sense of humor. There were stone tables and buildings. For whatever reason I had chosen an argument with him. Scolding him for something. We argued until we lay on the floor laughing. We laughed until our sides hurt and I rolled onto my side, pushing up onto my elbow to give myself leverage when I struck him in the stomach. It silenced his laughter immediately..."

"Wait," William broke in on the story and gave me a questioning look, "is your idea of warming a man up striking him?"

"No, not always." I shook my head and smiled, knowing what he was really asking. "Sometimes I just pounce on them."

"I shall remember that." Shaking his head he sat back in the chair.

"Well, he did not take kindly to being struck as hard as he was. He grabbed a hold of me and pulled me over him, rolling with me until he sat on my thighs. Laughing again that he had finally come out on top..." I let it trail off, smiling and thinking about it, but not sure how far to go with the story. Taking another sip of the bitter liquid.

"Go on!" Mary giggled an encouragement. "Tell us!"

"I let him end up on top, I could have moved him should I have had the idea to move him. He stared at me until he stopped laughing, I began sending a feeling of excitement and playfulness to him through the contact of our bodies. He did not take the hint as easily as I thought he would, I ended up having to show him exactly what I meant. When we were finished, I stood up, telling him t'was time to go. He did not seem too excited about having to go anywhere. He later told me that it was different, not a normal activity that you find with everyone, but there was a different feeling about it. We remained friends, having a few more activities, until the day I left there."

"Why did you leave?" Mary asked, looking at me.

"Was my time to go." I shrugged, "t'was not as funny as you and William though." I laughed, watching as he sat up in his chair, resting his elbows on his knees and holding his cup between his hands.

"What did he mean different?" William asked.

Beth laughed, "she probably could teach us a trick or two is more then likely what she meant."

"Did I ask you?" William smiled at her.

"I could teach them a trick or two, but we would need a male willing to be the test subject." I grinned at him.

"Is that a question?" he looked at me, and then at the other two. We all burst into another round of laughter at the look on his face, he was genuinely curious if I had meant it as a question.

"You look tired." Mary laid her head on the back of the chair and looked down at me.

"A little." I had only made it half way through my cup and I was ready to pass out, my head hurt slightly and my eyes kept drifting shut as I laid my head onto my arm on the chair. "Maybe more than a little."

"I have a spare room you could take for the night." Beth offered.

"Tis it night already?" William stood up looking out the window.

"Yes, we have been in here most of the day. Oh how time passes when you least see it." Beth stood up, "the room is at the end of the hall to your right William, you can see her there and stay if you like. Come on Mary, coins to make before the night is done with." She smiled at Mary and waved towards her.

"Yes, many many coins to make before the sun rises!" Mary hopped up, careful not to jar me as my head began to spin from the voices and movements around me.

It was not so much the movements physically that sent me into a swirl, but the movements of everyone's energies around me. I felt their moods and their movements, it made a spinning environment in the room.

"You asleep?" William stood over me.

"Not yet." I tried shaking my head which just sent it into a wave of that uneasy feeling that comes with drinking of the rotten fruit, creating a twisting feeling in the pit of your stomach.

"Let's get you to a bed before you fall asleep here." He set his cup on the table in the room, bending and reaching down towards me. He held onto my arms, helping me to stand up. "Are you okay?"

"Tis not smart to drink rotten fruit when you are as different as I am." I couldn't balance my feet underneath me, I chose to stand still with my eyes close and lean on him as it felt as if the floor was spinning under me.

"Okay..." He let the statement trail off and stood there like a post holding me up for a moment. "Can you walk?"

"Yes Sir." I tried walking forwards with my eyes closed which only seemed to increase the spinning feeling. My legs felt as if they were missing the bones of support in them, as if they were just flesh and tissue.

"No you can not walk." William stopped, stopping me as he did so.

"Maybe not." I admitted, opening my eyes slightly we had just barely made it out of the room.

"So you do not fall over the rail." He offered his reason as he reached around behind me. Lifting me at my knees, the other arm around my back. I felt him begin to move again, felt the movement in his muscles and energy. Closing my eyes I laid my head against his chest. "Almost there." I heard his voice through the mist of my own mind, as well as the sound of his foot hitting the bottom of the door, pushing it open.

"Here." I told him as I sensed the change in his energy change from one of carrying me to how to set me down.

"Yes." He bent slightly, lowering me down towards the bed, pulling the blanket out from under my body as I rolled onto my side, snuggling into the head rest and closing my eyes. He laid the blanket back over me, "I will return in a moment." I heard him walk towards the other side of the room and fell asleep.

Chapter Forty-one

Waking up I found myself snuggled up against William as close as I could get. My head tucked into the curve of his arm and my arms pulled up in front of me between my body and his, the blanket was pulled up around us. The room was dark with the curtain pulled over the window and no fire for light or warmth in the room. There wasn't a sound coming from anywhere outside of the room, as if everyone was sleeping in this morning. Turning over and putting my back to him, debating whether to get up or not, only caused him to roll with me, throwing his arm over, I rolled my eyes realizing my decision had been made for me. I was staying in bed, otherwise I would be waking him up.

'*Now there is an idea...*' I thought to myself, smiling as I planned out the idea to completion. '*I could roll him off the bed and fall on him, he would be injured not only from hitting the floor but from me jumping on him.*' Beginning to giggle at the idea of the look that would come over his face almost had me acting on it, but that would just be a little too mean. '*Or I could crawl on top of him and start transferring images to his head, feelings, thoughts. Play with him a bit before rolling him from the bed... The possibilities are endless...*' I continued to debate with myself the best process of waking a man who seemed dead to the world at the moment.

Finally deciding on playing games, I had to bite my own lip to keep from laughing aloud. Sliding his arm from my side as he rolled onto his back, rising up onto my knees, careful not to move or jar the bed any for risk of waking him before it wasn't time, I beat the laughter down as I watched him sleeping, laying flat on his back now. He must have had a good deal to drink the night before to be out as deeply as he was at this moment. Moving slowly until my knees were almost right up against him, I lifted the blanket gently and managed to move my right knee over his hips before letting the blanket back down. There was barely a half inch between his lap and myself in this position as I leaned forward, resting my chest against his and my elbows on the pillow next to his head. Moving my right hand so it could tickle his cheek and behind his ear I watched as the facial muscle began to twitch and had to stop and beat the laughter back down inside before I continued by playing with his hair and ear. Touching just enough for his nerves to feel it but not quite hard enough to wake him just yet.

    It finally hit me after a few more minutes of watching his face twitch under my finger, I remembered where we were and what this place was. *'That's it!'* I thought.

    I lowered myself down against him completely and leaned forward and began to blow softly on his neck, putting my lips as close I could to his neck, right below his ear, without touching him. Feeling him begin to stir slightly under me, I moved my hands around and placed one onto his arm and the other on his head, sending soft shocks of energy into him. I felt his hand begin to wonder up my thigh and again had to bite my lips closed to keep from giggling, his eyes were still closed and he hadn't realized just who was sitting on him yet. As his other hand began running up and down my other thigh along with the first, he turned his head slightly in the direction mine was in. As I felt his lips begin kissing my neck I couldn't hold it in any longer and began laughing hysterically. As his eyes flew open and he saw me, the shock washed over his face, and I fell off of him back onto the bed, continuing to laugh and giggle as my eyes began watering.

    "Damn woman!" He grumbled, sitting up in the bed and

wrapping the blanket around his middle, stalking off towards an adjacent, smaller room.

I continued to lay in the bed laughing until I could no longer see as I heard him mumbling and cursing in the other room. Hearing a bang almost immediately followed by another round of cursing, and thud that was followed by a yelp. My sides hurt so much as the pains began to spread across my stomach and my lungs felt as if they could not get enough oxygen into them. I moved towards the end of the bed, intending on standing up but just as I went to sit up in the bed I heard a crash come from the room which sent me into another fit of giggles as I fell off the side of the bed and continued to lay laughing on the floor.

Chapter Forty-two

A few moments passed and I sensed him near me, looking up through the blurry vision of water in my eyes I saw him standing over me. Glaring down at me, I tried to stifle the laughter from continuing as he assumed a less than pleasant stance.

"Are you done?" He asked, watching me as I lay on the floor.

"Yes... maybe..." I almost starting laughing again because of the look on his face, snarling almost as he glared at me.

"Must you do those things?" He reached down, extending his hand to help me up from the floor.

"Yes." I took hold of his hand as he pulled me to my feet, sitting back down on the bed.

He sat next to me, shaking his head, "tis not nice to do."

"I am not a nice person." I chuckled, wrapping my arm around his middle and leaning against him. "But I do have a sense of humor."

"HA!" He exclaimed as he turned his head to look at me, "that is not a sense of humor, that is torture in the worst form."

"How do you mean?" I asked him, trying to stay serious.

"You do not wake a man in that way unless you plan on... unless there is to be activities afterwords, and laughing at him as he wakes up is torture because he knows you will not partake in the activities."

"Your point?" I smiled, knowing full well what I had done and feeling quite proud of myself.

"My point is that you can only do it so often, continuing to do it leaves pains in a man!"

"Tis not my problem."

"Yes it is." He smiled finally, pushing me back on the bed as he laid onto his side. "I may want you to exchange something for the cost of the drink last night."

"I only had half a cup, so I owe you not a thing." I slapped his stomach.

"If that is all it takes to keep you from throwing yourself on the bed I may have to give it to you by the night so I may sleep."

"There is always the floor." I leaned up on an elbow and looked at him. "You do not have to torture yourself by sleeping in the bed with me, you may sleep on the floor."

"Tis warmer with a body next to you."

"Again it is not my problem. Your warmth is your own concern, not mine." I was purposely being antagonizing.

"See if I let you curl up next to me as a cat does again! I will not keep you warm any more." He chuckled.

"I do not need your body to stay warm, I will just steal your blanket and add it to my own."

"And you would lose that hand you like to use to wake a man with!"

"Try it and you may lose your arm." I gave him a serious look. "Or you may find it broken in two."

I started to pull on the short hairs on his chest and stomach, pulling them just enough to become taunt and pull at the skin. William began slapping at my hand as I continued to do it, from where his ribs met his breastbone down to where his pants tied just below his belly button.

"Would you stop it!" He grabbed my hand.

"Make me." I smiled at him, moving so I could sit on my legs and use my other hand to continue pulling at the hairs.

"Alright." Chuckling he grabbed for my other hand, missing it as I jerked it away.

Wrestling against his grip on my other hand I crawled back onto his stomach and sat on him, forcing the air out of his lungs as I let my weight drop onto him just below the breastbone. As he let go of my hand and tried to catch his breath I began using both hands to tickle him, finding those spots that can't stand to be touched on his sides.

"Stop it!" He laughed at me, trying to move his torso as I squeezed with my legs and laughed back at him.

Grabbing my hands he finally managed to force his torso upright, sliding me down until I sat in his lap. I could feel him, already starting to grow harder as my backside rested against him. His energy was growing hot with lust, he was forcing himself to behave. Laughing he pulled my arms around behind my back, "remember what happened in the meadow?" I reminded him of how he was thrown away from me.

"Do not care." He smiled at me, holding my hands behind my back.

"Let my hands go and I will show you something." I became serious, no longer laughing or smiling, but fully intending on showing him something I was sure he had never experienced.

"Okay." He let go of them, watching me as if I was going to attack him like a wild animal.

Bringing my hands around I placed them on his shoulders, "close your eyes." I watched as he closed them and then closed my own eyes. I began concentrating on sending what I felt over the connection, showing him exactly what and how I felt sitting in his lap, both physically felt from him and what I felt inside. His thighs under my butt, his manhood straining against me, his hands on my back, the heat of his body as it came off of him. The heat from my own body and the tingling inside, the moisture beginning to build between my hips.

"Is that..." he tried to form a question.

"That is what I feel." I finished his question by answering it.

"That is... new..." He laughed at the wording he had chosen to describe it.

"Now feel this, both as yourself and as me." I whispered,

putting my lips against his and letting him feel what it felt like to experience both sides at once. The way his lips felt against mine, the sensations it caused inside of me, almost like sparks passing between our lips.

As I continued to deepen the contact, sliding my tongue into his mouth until I could taste him, he pulled away, catching his own breath. "Amazing." Was the only thing he was able to say.

"Imagine that while your having activities." I laughed at him, removing my hands and the connection.

"You mean... you can do that while you're... ahem... you know?" He titled his head, watching me.

"Yes I can." I nodded.

"Is it an offer?" He smirked.

"Maybe." I tried not to laugh, it was beginning to get hard not to laugh at the situation again.

"What do I have to do to turn it into an offer?" He started to turn red in his cheeks again.

"I do not know." I shrugged, wrapping my hands around his neck until they could touch one another.

"Maybe... this..." He moved slightly, placing his mouth against my neck and gently kissing down from my hair line to the neck line of the dress. Sliding his hands over my back, almost as if he was working the knots out of it.

"That might do it." I laughed, almost moaning from the sensations, moving my hands until they slid under his arms and the palms rested on his back, sending the connection through again. As his energy changed I could tell that he felt every movement he made as I felt it, as he felt it.

Turning his torso sideways, he wrapped his arms around my back and leaned over, moving his legs up unto the bed, his knees between my thighs as he moved upwards, watching me as I watched him. Pushing the neckline of the dress aside he began kissing his way from the side of my neck to my shoulder. Moving my hands onto his shoulder's, making the connection again. As we felt his hand slide down my side, onto the thigh, we could feel it as he moved it under the skirt of the dress, touching skin as he slid the skirt upwards, brushing his hand over my thigh, the callouses on his hands as it touched the smooth skin on my hip, pulling me closer to him. He could feel himself as he let his weight down, laying his hips against my own, the pants as they scratched against my bare skin. He could feel the bulge straining against them as I felt it, pressing against this bodies virgin territory. He felt the reaction of my body, the way it tensed and released, the moisture building inside as the tingling grew harder to ignore between my legs.

"God..." he chuckled, laying his forehead against my shoulder.

"Hm?" I laughed.

"I can not concentrate on a damn thing." I felt the laughter roll through his body.

"You mean... wait, this is not normal?!" I mocked him.

Laughing, "no, this is not normal."

"Told you I could teach them tricks." I began mocking him

again.

"Can I... is it possible for me to show you what I feel?" He leaned up, looking down at me, completely serious in his question.

"Not likely. You are not like me, would take you a while to learn to do it." I shrugged.

"Too bad." He took a hold of my hands, holding them down against the bed, moving his mouth against mine.

As his tongue slid inside, dancing with mine I began sending the connection through our hands again. Not only physical feelings, but other senses as well. The way his tongue tasted, the smells as I smelt them, the sound of his heartbeat as I heard the blood coursing through him. As his body began to move instinctively, rocking it's hips against mine almost as if part of his body sought the area the cloth prevented it from touching. He felt the way my muscles tightened each time I felt his hard bulge rub against the bare skin of my entrance, the heat rising from the base of me as he moved against me and was forced to stop, catching his breath.

"I do not think it can be done this way..." he sighed, chuckling again. "Too much at once, I cannot think, I cannot act, I cannot concentrate on anything, even my own mind."

"Yes it can." I smiled at him, trying not to laugh at the reaction he was having, it was perfectly natural to react that way the first time. It was true, it overloaded the senses at first, but once you let the bodies do what nature had bred into them, it was not hard. Raising my hips against him until I could feel his member pushing against me I whispered my instructions to him, "Just follow your instincts, do whatever your body wants, let your body go where it wants."

"But..." he was cut off as the door to the room came open.

"Are ye up yet?!" The man yelled as he stepped inside.

William dropped his forehead against my chest momentarily as he sat back on his knees, pulling the skirt of the dress back down over my legs as I laughed at the interruption. The man was one I had seen before, the one who had asked me to leave the barracks when William was hurt. The look on his face was almost pure horror, a mix of curiosity showed in the expression as well, his cheeks were just as red as William's.

"Do you mind?" William glared at him, shaking his head.

"Beth said you stayed here last night..." The man turned his back to us, standing in much the same spot as he had when he was looking at us. "I thought... maybe... well you were passed out from the drink the night before. I came to wake you for work as I have done before."

"I am not passed out, although I wish I was." William mumbled, getting out of the bed he pulled his shirt over his head.

"Should I return at a later time?" The man almost laughed.

"No." Bending, William picked his boots up from the floor, turning towards me he mouthed, "sorry."

"Are we decent?" The man asked, peeking over his shoulder.

"Head forward." William pushed on the man's back, "and out with you."

"Good morning!" I yelled at them, laughing. Almost hating

the man for interrupting, wishing he had not come in, I was beginning to enjoy myself. But on the other hand, it may have been good that he interrupted when he did, I did not know this bodies cycle yet.

William gave me a look and waved a hand at me as he walked out of the room, closing the door behind him as he pushed the man bodily out of the room.

Chapter Forty-three

I laid there in the bed, arms resting out to my sides, staring at the cloth that hung over the top. Taking note that between the posts on the sides there was a piece of wood connection them, almost like the frame of the bed was up top, it held the cloth that hung over it as well. Replaying the incident over in my mind, the man had walked in and seemed more shocked than anything to find William in the position he did. The look on that man's face had been worth the interruption. Rolling over I stared for a while at the soft light filtering through the curtain into the room. Sighing, as I rolled back over to the edge and sat up, I decided it was time to stop laying around. *'Surely there must be something to do in this town.'*

Pulling my shoes on as I stood up, I headed out of the door and left it open behind me. Beth had said that if a door was open it was okay for someone to go in, and since I was no longer in there it was okay for someone to go in. But that man had come in even with the door closed, they needed to implement the planks in this place so no one was bothered while they were occupied.

As I came to the bottom of the steps Beth called over, "Want something to eat?"

"Might as well." I walked over and sat down in one of the chairs at the bar.

"What do you want?" She leaned on the bar top in front of

me.

"Just any raw vegetable or fruit you have around." Smiling at her she nodded. Walking off a short ways and into a section under the stairs she returned with some of what she had. "How much do I owe you?"

"Nothing dear. Women are always welcome here free of charge. Besides, tis not everyday I get to hear William trampling one of my rooms and cursing." She laughed.

"You heard that huh?"

Nodding at me she smiled, "what did you do to him girl?"

"I had done nothing yet." I laughed.

"Nothing?" Mary plopped down on the chair next to me.

"Nothing... I had woke him up and he began falling around the adjacent room to the one we were in." I answered, chewing on an orange vegetable while I smiled.

"How did you wake him up though?" Beth looked me over as if I had done something even if I thought it was nothing.

"Crawled on his lap and teased him until he realized it was me."

"You are mean!" Mary nudged into me.

"T'was what he said... after yelling '*damn woman*' and getting out of bed, that's when you heard the crashing sounds of his stumbling. He cursed quite a bit until he returned to the room." I laughed remembering the look on his face, "he did not think it was as funny as I did."

"Ha! Most men do not!" Mary laughed while Beth smiled.

"I hear I admitted to where he was too soon?" Beth was encouraging me to continue.

"Just a little. The man walked in just in time to bring everything to a halt. I was apologizing for the teasing earlier."

"How? Details darling, details!" Mary nudged me again.

"I was showing him my tricks. And was willing to let it continue beyond..." I was not sure what term they used for what we were doing. "What do you call it? Before you do the deed but you are getting close?"

"Oh... we call it playing, but you can call it any number of things from teasing to warming up." Beth offered with a chuckle.

"Well, warming up we were, and I was half tempted to let it go further. But the man walked in, I swear he was more shocked than anything else!"

"I do not doubt that. He is used to coming in to haul William off and finding him asleep." Mary smirked.

"He said as much, wanted to know if he should return later." I laughed, "although I do think he would have stood there the rest of the day if he thought he could."

"Sir Henry is that way... he tends to be more a watcher than a player." Beth shrugged, handing me a cup of water to wash the vegetation down that I had been chewing on.

"So what are you doing today?" Asked Mary.

"I do not know, what is there to do in this town?" I looked at her.

"Mary, take the girl out and show her around." Beth sighed and then warned Mary, "and do not torture the men while you are out! I do not want the entire town in here tonight."

"I would never!" Mary placed her hand over her chest and batted her eyelashes.

"Yes you would and you have!" Beth began shooing us away from the bar, waving her hands at us to leave.

"Come on, lets have some fun!" Mary grabbed my arm and hooked it with hers as she led me out the front door.

Chapter Forty-four

We walked out of the woman's house and strolled down the street, arm in arm while she gave looks to various men just beginning their days. Giggling each time one shook his head or looked like he was going to faint from embarrassment, a few of them even made a weird sign over their chests and heads.

"What is that man doing?" I whispered to her when another man made that sign over himself.

Laughing she looked at me like I was joking, realizing I wasn't she tried to explain, "he believes he is protecting himself from me and my *evil* ways by making the sign of the cross over himself. The church has a lot of these people believing that playtime is evil and that we," she pointed to herself and smiled, "who earn coins from it are evil as well for doing so."

"He thinks that little," I tried imitating the sign as I laughed, "is going to protect him?"

"Absolutely. Little does he know his son John has already been in the house with a few of the girls." She gave me a knowing look. "But we do not tell him okay? He would probably die on the spot if he knew."

"Okay." I laughed.

"In here..." She pulled on my arm, pulling me inside of a

building.

"What is this place?" I asked, looking around I saw various cloths of different colors hanging around and a number of corsets hanging on a separate wall.

"Dress shop." She offered as she began looking over a few of the corsets. "We can buy the corsets ready made, and the cloth for our dresses from here so we can make them back where we live." She looked around us and leaned closer to me, whispering, "they don't make the kind of dresses we wear."

"What is wrong with the dresses you wear?" I looked her up and down, besides the fact that her skirt seemed to be permanently up around her thigh on one side and her breasts almost fell from her top she looked fine to me.

"Too much skin for the taste of most of the townsfolk. Might damage their minds or something." She held up a lacy corset that had a white backing to it and threads over the front of it making the lace. "This would go so well over a dress on you!"

"No... no no and no!" I laughed, shaking my head and my hands. "I wore one of them once and tis like torture, not again!"

"Tis not as bad when it is over your dress. I have the perfect dress to go with it back in my room, you will see." She handed it to me giggling, "hold this please."

"Fine." I shook my head at her, chuckling as she continued to look through the fabrics.

Some felt silky and sleek while others felt scratchy and thick, and then there were others that felt light and were almost see through. Taking a few of the light and seemingly see through from where they hung she hung onto my arm and pulled me towards a man standing at the other side of the building.

"Back again I see..." he looked from her to me, "new girl?"

"No, I am just showing her around since the people in this town are so unfriendly!" She had a mocking tone to her statement.

"Do not begin with me Mary. We all know how friendly you are, there is no need to flaunt it around the town and frighten the young men!" He laughed, shaking his head and counting the items she had handed to him, the fabrics and the corset. "5 gold."

"Pricy! I will have to work twice as hard to replenish what you are taking from me..." she gave him a look and leaned forward, "unless you care to take something else as payment."

I just about choked on my own tongue at the way she made eyes at him and spoke to him. Turning around so my back was to them I let the laughter bubbling up out.

"Taxes are coming up sweet girl, I need the coins more than I need... anything else right now." He laughed too.

"Fine, here you go. Maybe next time." She picked up the cloth and corset and grabbed my arm again, pulling me out of the building into the bright street again. As she pulled me towards another area of the street where a group of women stood with girls that seemed between the ages of 12 and 17 years she leaned over, giggling again, "watch this." Smiling at me she walked up to the women, "good day! And how are our men doing today, have I seen any of them lately?"

I almost fell over laughing as the women scrambled to cover their daughters ears and attempted to block their eyes at the same time. Their mouths hanging open as they gaped at Mary who only laughed and walked away.

"And they say I am mean!" I laughed out.

"I never said I was any better." Shrugging as she hooked her free arm back in mine again.

"Let us go back to the building before you are burnt for your tongue!" I remembered William's warnings to me to watch my tongue around these people.

"Oh don't be silly! These people know me all too well. I do this almost once a week, and most days I sit outside the woman's house and make eyes with every man that passes."

"You wench!" I slapped her arm and laughed.

"Do not forget it!" She laughed.

As we walked back to the woman's house she gave several more men looks, even a few Knights who were out in town, either riding or leading their horses. Reaching the door we walked in, Beth gave her a look and just laughed and shook her head as we headed up the staircase.

Chapter Forty-five

We spent the rest of the morning and into the early evening in Mary's room, talking and trading stories as she picked up various items of clothing from her floor. She tried convincing me more than once that I should put the dress on with the corset over the top.

"Which one?" I finally gave in, sitting on the chair in her room.

"Wait here..." she giggled hopping off towards where she had several dresses hanging. Fumbling through them while she talked to herself, debating over colors and necklines, heights and sleeve lengths.

"The decision is not that hard. Grab one so I can take it back off as soon as possible." I rolled my eyes, almost laughing at the way she was taking her time to make a decision, as if the rest of her day and night depending upon this decision alone.

"This!" Exclaiming as she turned around, holding up a dress that had a mix of colors on it. The bodice was a cream color while the skirt was a darker tan color, the thread through the hems of the dress were a bright green color. The neckline dropped lower than the one William had forced me to wear and the sleeves of the dress were almost non-existent as they seemed to be straps. It laced up the front instead of the back as well.

"Let us do this so we can remove it as quickly as possible." I stood up, untying the loop of the laces in the back of the dress I wore.

"This dress should go well with the corset we bought." She giggled while walking over towards me as I dropped the dress to the floor.

"Over my head or up from the bottom?" I wanted to know if it made a difference how the dress went on.

"Either way is fine, might be easier from the bottom though." She bent over, holding the dress down so I could step into it. "You do have hips on you!" She laughed as we had to loosen the laces to get the dress over my hips.

"T'was not my fault!" I laughed, pulling the dress up. Planning on positioning the shoulder straps after I had laced it back up part way I ran the threads through the eyelets on the dress up to the neckline that was more of a chest line on the dress.

"No... those do not go on your shoulders, they hang off onto your arms." She stopped me when I moved to adjust the straps up to my shoulders.

"How does it stay up then?" I looked at her, chuckling at the idea of the dress falling off at any moment.

"The corset keeps it in place." She smiled, grabbing the torture device off of her bed and unlacing it. "This laces up the front as well. Makes it easier to put on if you have no one to help" She held it out for me to look at, I took note of the fact that it lacked shoulder straps as well.

"How tight must it be to stay up?" I looked it over as she

wrapped it around my middle.

"Not that tight. We don't have to choke you with it, those women who do that are just asking for pain. We don't want our toys," she jiggled her top half giggling, "flattened to our chests as they seem to want."

"Hm..." I nodded, beginning to re-lace the corset up the front. It came to just below where the dress's neckline stopped.

"Now..." standing back she looked me over as if inspecting, "...hold still, don't move!" She turned around and rummaged through a drawer in her dresser. Holding white colored ribbon as she turned back around she grabbed the edge of the skirt and pulled it up on one side, tying it so that it hung just above my knee.

"What..." I tried to ask what she was doing.

"Just hold on!" She laughed, cutting me off as she turned back around and pulled out a cream colored skirt that had no top to it, "put this under the skirt of dress."

Pulling it up and underneath it hung in a contrast to the skirt of the dress, creating a simple but somewhat decent accent to the actual dress itself. "That is not as bad as I thought it would be."

"I know how to dress." She smiled at me, "now for that hair!"

"What is wrong with my hair?" I looked at her, almost laughing at the fun she was having.

"Sit down and let me work!" She shook her head as she pointed to a chair in front of the dresser. "Up or down?"

"Does not matter." I shook my head as she pulled it up and let it down again.

"Both then." She pulled part of my hair up and pinned it in place with a fragment of wood that had been laying on the top of the dresser.

"Now can we take this all of?" I looked back at her.

"No... keep it on for now. Will drive Sir William mad." She laughed.

"Always the tease?"

"Are we not all that way?" Raising an eyebrow as she smiled at me. "Besides, you might as well frustrate him further, was quite amusing this morning to listen to the clattering around he did."

"Yes it was." I laughed.

"Tis a new side of him, I think I like it. Not often you can disturb a man so that he falls over himself." She was still giggling, I could see that she was planning something by the look she had in her eyes.

Chapter Forty-six

"What?" I asked, sensing the difference in her, I was positive she was planning something now.

"We should play a game..." she got a serious look on her face.

"What kind of game?"

"Sir William will return this night to find you, he left you here and will return to the last place he knew you were at. Come down stairs with me, in that," she nodded at me, "dress. Work the floor with me, not really *working* but play along. When he comes in, I promise his mouth will drop."

"Why?" I laughed, knowing it would be fun but not sure why she was suggesting it.

"Because, there is something about you he likes. Will drive him mad." She shrugged, turning away and heading for the door, glancing back at me and smiling as she waved me along.

"Only tonight though, and I will not be seen in any mans lap or offering favors." I thought over any possible problems, trying to foresee anything that could happen. "If one is out of line, I will break him in two and leave him on your floor."

"Fine, fine." She hugged me to her side, laughing.

Laughing I walked with her down the stairs and looked around the building. There were a dozen or more men in the building tonight, several girls all dressed in revealing clothing, corsets on the outside of their dresses. Beth was behind the bar pouring drinks and setting cups with jugs down on trays before one of the girls took it. As our feet hit the bottom step I stopped and glanced at the door as it opened, William was coming in, smiling as he joked with a few of the Knights I had seen from the barracks. He watched his step, watched where he put his feet.

"Be brave girl." Mary whispered into my ear, giggling as she walked off, heading straight for the group of Knights who walked in with William.

Standing there, I felt odd, out of place for the first time since coming in here. Watching from a distance as the girls interacted with the men, pouring them drinks. Keeping an eye on William as he walked from the door to the bar where Beth was, how he hardly looked up at all. Almost as if he was still unsure of himself when he walked in here, still respectful of the women who worked here. Leaning on the top of the bar I saw him talking to Beth who nodded my direction.

Looking up from the bar which he had been staring at while talking to Beth, I watched him as he looked from my feet up over the skirt of the dress, the corset, stopping as his eyes finally met mine that were watching him. He continued to lean on the bar with one arm, staring as if he was looking through me, unblinking and unmoving. Beth laughed, leaning across the bar and nudging him, saying something to him which brought his head around to look at her. Chuckling, he nodded before pushing from the bar and walking towards the stairs where I still stood.

Stopping in front of me he looked me up from my feet again, "where did you get the dress?"

"Mary." I watched his cheeks begin to tint again.

"And the um..." pointing towards my stomach, "...the corset?"

"Mary bought it today."

"I see."

"I sure hope you can see." I smiled at him.

"And is there a reason for this?" He began to smirk.

"Not that I am aware of."

"You are not... I mean, your not going to work here?" His curiosity was getting the better of him.

"No. In fact," I stepped down, holding my hands behind my back and leaning towards him until my arm touched his, "I threatened to break any man who did not behave in half."

Glancing down at me as I smiled at him and walked off, it took a moment before he turned to follow me. Leaning forward as we walked until his mouth was near my ear he whispered to me. "Then why?"

"Because t'will drive you mad I am told." I turned my head to smile at him as he stopped.

Shaking his head he took the two steps to bring himself beside me again, "and if it does not work?"

"Then... I may have to wake you again as I did this morn." I looked from him to Beth behind the bar, "cup of water?"

"Sure thing." Beth smiled at me, handing me a cup of water from behind the bar as she looked to William. "And for you?"

"Hops... and a lot of it. I feel I may be needing it before the night is over." He stared at me, trying to figure out what my plan was, trying to plan around what he assumed my plan was.

"Will do you no good." I turned on my seat to look at him.

"What will do no good?" He looked confused.

"To stare at me like that. You cannot read my mind, nor anticipate anything I should do."

"Why not?" He took a swig of the hops as soon as Beth set it down in front of him.

"Because I plan as I go, not before, but as I act I plan."

"Where is your other dress?" He tried to keep his eyes looking at my face.

"In Mary's room." I laughed, realizing just what she meant when she had said it would drive him mad. He was trying as hard as he could to keep eye contact and not glance down. His own mind betrayed him in it's curiosity and wonder, but he tried to be respectful enough.

"Beth..." He looked over his shoulder towards Beth who was standing behind the bar watching, and listening, trying to prevent the smile from creeping onto her face. "How much do I owe you for the room last night, and tonight?"

"Oh... honey..." she leaned over and patted him on the back, "...thy thrashing around was payment enough. Brought many of the girls a laugh today."

His head shot up as he stared at her, mouth gaping open as he realized what she was referring to. Reaching a finger over I placed it under his chin, pushing upwards and closing his mouth and smiling as he looked at me, "tis not polite to hang ones mouth to the floor."

"I am receiving lessons from a wench and a.... what are you anyway?" He shook his head, chuckling.

"I am, only that, that I am." I wiped any expression from my face as he tried to figure out the meaning behind my words.

"Take him up to the break room dear." Beth handed me a jug, "be sure he does not pass out. Would not like to mistakenly send someone to retrieve him again."

"Aye, would be a bad idea." I took hold of the handle on the jug and the handle on my cup, standing up I smiled at Beth. "Thank you."

"Just be sure to send him into the stumbles again in the morn, brings smiles to peoples faces to hear, t'will be thanks enough." She waved us off.

William was still hanging onto his cup, staring at the bar and pondering over his own thoughts. "You coming?" I bumped my hip into his thigh.

"Hm?" He looked at me briefly before shaking his head again, lifting his cup. "I am coming. Lead the direction."

"I seem to always lead the direction, tell you what..." I handed the jug to him, "you carry this and you go first so I may watch you walk away for a change."

He smirked, and then realized what I meant by the statement and shook his head again. But he did not refrain from following my directions, he carried the jug and led the way to the staircase, walking up it carefully step by step so as not to spill a drop from the jug or his cup. I watched him, a few steps behind, looking him over in much the same way he had looked me over on more than one occasion. As he reached the top he glanced back, to which I only smiled, as he began walking off again, down the hall and into the break room. Setting the jug down as well as himself onto the same chair he had occupied the night before. Setting the cup of water down next to the jug I plopped onto the long chair I had sat in part of the night before.

Chapter Forty-seven

We sat there for some time without saying anything. He stared at his hands that wrapped around his cup, as if by staring at it, it would turn into something else. I watched him, legs curled up beside me as I leaned on the back of the chair, waiting for him to say something or at least drink what he had ordered.

"What are you thinking?" I couldn't stand the silence in the room any longer, not even the noise from downstairs was enough.

"Not a thing." He looked up at me, somber and relaxed.

"You have been quiet for some time, there is nothing in your mind?"

"No." He shook his head.

"What did you do today?" I laid my head down onto my arm that was sitting atop the chair's back.

"Same as any other day. Made sure the boys had their duties done, some training. Made sure the men continue to work and see to their duties." He shrugged.

"Nothing different?"

"No. Well, maybe one thing different." He smirked.

"Hm." I closed my eyes.

"And you?"

"Went into town with Mary, watched as she shopped for cloth and corsets and then bothered some of the towns women and their daughters. Watched as she taunted various men of varying ages." I smiled.

"Ah... so you had a full day?" He joked.

"Aye, I did. Spent the afternoon and early evening trying to dissuade her from this dress on me, but as you can see I gave in."

"Yes, I can see that."

"At least it is not as uncomfortable as the one you had placed me in."

"How is that?"

"In yours I was forced to wear the corset under it and have it tight enough that I could not breath." I opened my eyes and straightened my head to look at him, "in this one, the corset is not tight and it is not on the inside to bruise my flesh."

"Did the other bruise you?" He was concerned he may have tightened it too much.

"No, but felt as if it would... may have if it had stayed on any longer."

"Tell me of where you come from. The people, the life..." He grew curious.

"So you were thinking?" I smiled, "is there anything specific you would like to know?"

"Yes, I admit I was thinking. But no, nothing specific, anything you wish to tell will be fine." He finally took a drink, sliding down in the chair slightly as he got more comfortable.

"Well... we do not form family groups, children are raised by the entire village, or town. They run, they play everywhere and everyone helps in instructing them."

"Do they have parents?"

"Yes, they have genetic donors."

"What is ge-net-ick?" He was not familiar with the term.

"Genetic is your blood. When you cut yourself, you see the red color it makes as it runs out. But what you cannot see is smaller, individual pieces of that red blood. Those are your genetics." I tried to explain it. "You pass those on to your offspring, they are both half yourself and half of the other person. In our world, parents are genetic donors, they give the genetics to create a child, and while they foster the child in most cases, the children are raised by all the people. Instructed, taught, scolded, loved."

"Do you have genetic donors?"

"Yes, I have a female who donated part of her genetics, and a male who donated a portion of his... here I am as a result of that."

"But they are not..." he was thinking of what he wanted to ask and how to put it, creases showing in his forehead as he tried to put it into terms. "They are not the only ones who raise you? You do not call them mother or father?"

"No, I call them by their names. They are known as my genetic donors, it is recorded, but what you think of as parents are not the same as what we have."

"Do you have any sisters, brothers?"

"Two full brothers, much older than I am. A sister on the males side, older than both myself and my brothers."

"How do you consider them brothers and sisters, if you do not consider the parents to be a mother or father?"

"Those terms are ones you are familiar with. I see them as genetic matches. The two *brothers* are a complete genetic match as they share the same donors. The *sister* is a partial genetic match as she only shares one of the same donors." It actually seemed complicated when trying to explain it to someone.

"Hm..." he nodded, acknowledging that he understood, at least part of it. "Do they do what you do?"

"What do you mean?" I laid my head back down on my arm.

"I mean, you have stated you are a warrior, you have taught others to fight. Are they warriors as well?"

"Oh... my brothers are. Both of them have been trained as such, one works in a land far off and the other is an instructor. He teaches others to fight. My sister, she is a genetic donor to one girl, and also works with plants."

"What plants do you have there? The same as here or are

they different?" He sat up straighter, leaning his elbows on his knees.

"Different, but close. Big, small, thin, wide, tall, short... the same as here, they come in all shapes and sizes, but they are slightly different." I could picture the different plants in my mind, but could not find the words to describe them. "Some grow fruits and vegetables, while others bare no vegetation for eating. There is water there, both fresh waters and seas with a higher content of undrinkable contents. There are animals of all different sizes and species, both in the waters and on the land, as well as in the sky's."

"Your buildings?"

"Made of smooth stone. White, or gray, sometimes you will find a building or parts of a building with various colors to them, made of different stones."

"Someday I would like to see it." He nodded, sitting back and taking another swig from his cup.

"Someday you might. I do not pretend to know what will happen in the coming times."

"If there was a chance, would you show me around?"

"Yes, if you come to see it one day, I will gladly show you around." I closed my eyes again, resting as I watched the images of my home flash in my mind.

"Are you tired?"

"Just a little."

"Want to retire for the evening?"

"Not yet."

"Will you fall asleep on the seat?"

"No."

"Okay." He let the conversation go, remaining in his chair and relaxing his tired body from the days work he had done. Leaving me be as I sat, leaning on the back of the long chair with my eyes closed, relaxing my mind.

Chapter Forty-eight

"I think tis time we both went to sleep..." William touched my shoulder, I had dozed off. "Has been a long day."

"I guess so." Stretching as I stood up from the chair I remembered the dress I was wearing, "but first this thing must come off."

"I would help, but someone would walk in no doubt." Smiling as he knew with the run we had already had today, someone would walk through the door the moment he began helping.

"Yes, and then where would we be. I have to go find my other dress..."

"No, you do not." He interrupted, "I brought a clean shirt for you. Will be a better sleep in it, rather than a dress."

"And where did you carry it?" I did not remember seeing him carrying a shirt when he came in.

"Right here." He tugged at the shirt he had on.

"Off with it than!" I shook my head, unlacing the corset.

"Could we at least be in the room we are staying?" He looked around, at the open door and anywhere else but at me.

"Aye, we could, but will we?" I began feeling that urge to taunt him make it's way to the surface again.

"Go to the room, I will be there in a moment." He gave me a stern look, as if that alone was going to move me.

"You go, and I will be there in a moment." I put my hands on my hips, refusing to be ordered around.

"Fine." He set the jug and cup back down that he had picked up a second before. Turning towards me, bending, and lifting me up over his shoulder.

"Put me down!" I laughed. "Tis not fun to be hung upside down where you may be dropped on your head!"

"Then stop squirming and I will not drop you." He tightened his arm around my thighs as he left the room.

"Play nice!" I heard Mary's voice, glancing up she was laughing as she came up the stairs with a man who staggered behind her.

"I will as long as she does." William called back to her as I moved just enough to put my elbow on his back and rest my chin on my hand, rolling my eyes. Opening the door with his free hand, taking the few strides to the bed, and dropping me down on it before I knew what was happening he smiled and turned away from me.

"Just where do you think you are going?" I jumped up.

"Closing the door, or can you not see tonight?" He closed the door and turned around.

"I can see just fine, but would rather find a reason to scold you." I shrugged, smiling, "men require..."

"...scolding by the day, sometimes twice a day." He cut me off finishing my statement for me, "yes, I remember."

"So are you going to give me your shirt or must I sleep naked?" I resumed the process of unlacing the corset, pulling the ribbon like threads through the eyelets until I reached the bottom where I removed it completely. Grabbing the edge before it fell to the floor I tossed it onto the chair nearby.

"I am thinking over my previous offer, I may wish to keep my shirt so the hair on my body remains where it has grown." He watched the corset go from my hand to the chair, looking back at me.

"Then you will have other problems. Because my offer from this morn is no longer available, and I will have to sleep naked, which means you will be on the floor with no blanket."

"Fine." He grabbed the bottom of his shirt, pulling it over his head and tossing it in my direction. "You may have the shirt, but I am sleeping in the bed."

"Thank you." I smiled, irritating him further.

"T'would not kill you to put the offer back on the table." He bent over, pulling his boots off as he set them next to the door.

"Oh but it may." I laughed.

"Why do you think that?" He asked, walking towards the other side of the bed and to the window where he closed the curtain.

"Because I do not know the body's cycle yet." I began to unlace the front of the dress, laying his shirt on the bed as I did so.

"Cycle?" He turned around and looked at me.

"Yes, cycle. The female of the human species cycles by the month as the moon changes. Part of the month, they bleed. Part of the month, they can become with child."

"Yes, I know this, but why must you know *the* cycle of this body?" He sat down on the bed, one leg bent onto the bed as he watched me from behind.

"Because I wish to miss the fertility of this body. We do not want small versions of myself running around." I turned around, dropping the dress to my hips as I reached for his shirt.

"Oh..." he dropped his gaze down to the blanket laying on the bed, fiddling with the threads in it. "Does make sense."

"You can look now." I told him once the shirt was in place. It hung down to the middle of my thighs and was roomy, he was correct when he said it would be better sleeping than the dress.

"How long..." he paused, turning a red shade in his cheeks once again, "...until you know this cycle?"

"I will know once the body sheds, bleeds. Will not be hard to figure from there." I pushed the dress over my my hips and dropped it to the floor, stepping out and picking it up to lay on the chair as well.

"And when will that happen?" He stood back up, pulling the blanket down.

"I do not know." I crawled into the bed and under the blanket, "could be this night, could be weeks from now."

"Want me to start the fire?" He had his answer, standing next to the bed and watching while I pulled the blanket up to my chin.

"The blanket is just cold, needs to be warmed up. But if you wish to start it, that is fine."

"No... I would rather have a cat curled next to me for the night than you kicking the blanket from the bed along with myself." He laughed, sitting down on the edge and pulling the blanket back up.

"Well, if you want a cat next to you, lay yourself down so I may cuddle." I gave him a look that said everything else. On one hand, I was cold, on the other I wanted to go to sleep and he was taking his time in providing either heat or sleep.

"I am going to regret this." He slid down in the bed, shaking his head and laughing.

"You will, no doubt of this." I laughed, squirming over next to him and tucking my head into his side, my legs next to his and my arms between my chest and his ribs, closing my eyes it was almost immediate in the tiredness setting in.

As he moved his right arm around and laid his hand on my back, he leaned his head over and whispered, "good night."

Chapter Forty-nine

Waking in the early morning before the sun had risen, I was in much the same position as I had curled into the night before, so was William. The blanket was pulled around us though, tucked under my back and bum, between our bodies slightly, and by the tensions in it I assumed under his side as well.

"Cold?" He glanced down towards me.

"A little." I snuggled as close as I could, trying to draw out the heat in his body.

"Stay put." He removed his arm from around me and slid out of bed, careful not to disturb the blanket much.

I let my eyes follow him as he walked over to the fireplace, adjusting the logs in it and picking the flint from the stone near by up, starting a fire with the sparks from the fire-stone. He knelt a while longer, adjusting the logs on top until they began to burn. Straightening he walked into the adjacent room, carrying another blanket back with him as he came.

"Will help to keep us warmer until the fire heats the room." He smiled, throwing it over the top of the other blanket and myself.

"Hm..." I snuggled further down under the blankets that were now doubled on top of me until just my eyes peeked out from the top of them.

"You look like one of those shelled fish I have seen by the seas." He crawled back into bed, lifting the blankets only high enough to let himself in and setting them back down. He moved downwards until he was next to me, laying on his side as he watched me peek over the blankets at him. He smiled, "There are faster ways to warm your body up."

Moving slightly so my mouth came above the blankets I smiled back, "I am sure there are but we are not using those ways. Just move closer and I'll turn over, body heat along with the blankets and fire will work, just give it time." I turned over and pulled the blankets around the front of me.

"As you wish." He chuckled, sliding forward until his chest was flat with my back, wrapping his arm around the front of me and laying his head back down on the headrest.

Laying there, I fell back asleep, finally warming up from the cold chill that had set in on the room over night. It had never been this cold in Atlantis, nor Egypt. They were warmer and to the south of where I was now, a more stable climate. Knocking on the door brought me almost straight up out of the bed as it penetrated my sleep.

"Easy." William pushed me back down into the bed with a hand on my arm. "Tis just my man coming to raise me."

"Mhm..." I snuggled back down under the covers as he slid out of the bed, I planned to make use of the body heat he had left on the bed and blankets. I was watching, again with just my eyes peeking over the blankets as he walked towards the door, opening it slightly.

"Tis morning Sir. Storm clouds moving in, blocking the sun out." I heard the man on the other side of the door telling William what the weather was like and that it was indeed morning. Clouds would explain the lack of light filtering through the curtain.

"I will be out in a moment." William nodded and shut the door. Turning back towards where I lay in the bed he shook his head, laughing, "I am going to need that shirt."

"No." Was my muffled reply.

"Aye, I am. Storm is coming, I must be able to make it back to the barracks without catching a fever." He stood next to the side of the bed, waiting.

"If you must." I slid further under the blankets and began wiggling out of the shirt.

"What are you doing?" I heard him ask, half laughing as he watched me moving under the blankets.

"Getting your shirt for you without letting the warmth escape." I threw his shirt at him after I pulled it out from under the blankets where I had taken it off.

"You are not wearing anything under there." He smiled, catching his shirt as it hit him in the chest.

"No, and you must go to your duties." I tucked the blankets back around my neck, just under my chin, smiling at him.

"I must have done something bad to deserve this." Grumbling he pulled his shirt back on.

"To deserve what?"

"This torture. Continuous taunting. Having duties to attend

to while the woman I have slept with all night becomes naked." Shaking his head he walked back towards the door, reaching down as he pulled his boots on.

"Aye, you must have been a bad boy." I nodded, trying not to laugh at him.

"I agree." He glanced back, shaking his head again as he opened the door, "I will see you tonight."

"I will be right here unless it warms up." I snuggled further down into the bed until the blankets covered my nose. I could smell him on the blankets, feel the heat from where his body had been, it was enough to begin warming me once again and put me back to sleep.

Chapter Fifty

Waking up later in the morning, I sensed other people in the room, smiling to myself I recognized them as Beth and Mary before I even saw them, I could tell their energy without having to look at them. Popping my head out from under the covers I looked at them, standing next to the bed and looking down at me.

"Anything to share?" Mary dumped herself down into the bed next to me.

"What do you mean?" I rolled over, keeping the blankets over my shoulders.

"Well... apparently, according to Beth, William left in quite a hurried way. And not hurried of his own accord, but hurried by his friend. And here you lay til the late morning. Do you have anything you want to share?" Mary was like a little child conspiring with another over something they found of interest.

"Not a thing to share." It was the truth.

"Nothing at all?" Beth sat down in the chair, "he tried to turn around three times before his friend pushed him from the building this morning, there must be something!"

"I have no clothes on." I giggled, figuring that must be the reason, he had been bad and was being punished.

"And why have you no clothes on, hm?" Mary looked over the room as if looking for a clue.

"Because he needed his shirt back." I shrugged.

"Why were you in his shirt?" Beth looked at me. It was a woman's house after all, most of the women either slept in their dress or naked, not in the man's shirt.

"The dress, I did not want to sleep in it. He gave me his shirt so I would not be sleeping naked. He found need of it this morning so I gave it back and crawled down into the covers to stay warm."

"And he did not get to stay!" Mary exclaimed.

"No, he did not. Duties first." I smiled.

"And he did not finish last night what he had begun the morning before?" Beth was reserving judgment until after she knew everything.

"No he did not."

"He will surely burst!" Giggling, Mary loved the idea of him having to wait.

"Oh he may explode on someone... he believes he is being punished by having to see to his duties while I lay naked in the bed."

"Men are always being punished, or believe they are. Most times I tend to disagree with that statement, but it does seem to be true in this case." Beth finally laughed, sitting back in the chair and relaxing her head against the back of it.

"Why do you agree this time?" I looked from Beth to Mary, waiting for one of them to answer as they exchanged looks with each other.

"He comes, he goes. He never stays or has problem leaving here in the mornings. Yes he talks to us, jokes with us, but there is a difference in how he is acting as of late." Beth begin.

"Tis not just the reaction of being taunted either. He is playing along with what you are doing to him, letting it continue, enjoying it even, I might go as far to say." Mary continued.

"He does take his time with my new girls, but always on the night I send him up he breaks them so they may be of some use and make more coins by morning." Beth added.

"And he has spent how many nights near you? Alone? And still you remain unviolated." Mary looked at me.

I finally burst into laughter at the way they had obviously been discussing this before coming in this morning. I couldn't decide which was better, the entertainment I received by watching William be tortured, or the antics of these two.

"What do you laugh at? We are serious!" Beth was taken by the way I found the conversation humorous.

"I find it all funny." I took some deep breaths, relaxing now as I lay back on the head rests.

"How so?" Mary leaned down on her side.

"Well, first William *breaks* your girls because they want to be broke, they want to work here. He does it in one night because that is what they want. If they did not, he would not do it. Second, the man knows what I would do to him if he tried anything that I did not offer. I remain unviolated because I do not want a child, and do not know this bodies cycle, so he will wait until I do know or he will find himself in a hole." I shook my head, chuckling as I took a break in the speech. "I do not know which is funnier, watching him be tortured, or watching the two of you talk."

"We aim to please!" Mary giggled, finding the entire speech I had just given them amusing.

"And it gives us entertainment to watch the man walk around as if he was in two places at once." Beth added with a smile, "allows us something to talk about the rest of the day."

"If he only knew he may try to cover himself, block out what you two see." I laughed. "For a private man he wears his thoughts outside of himself much too often."

"Only as of late." Beth's smile grew bigger.

"He is bothered... hot... and ready... just waiting on the hankie to drop telling him to go!" Mary giggled.

"By the stars!" I grumbled, pulling the blankets back over my head at the idea of what she meant by that statement, I was not sure I wanted to know, and for the moment I did not want to know. The laughter at my reaction died out as they left the room, leaving me laying under the covers for a while longer.

Chapter Fifty-one

Finally giving up on going back to sleep, I threw the blankets down and stretched. Standing up, I wrapped one of the blankets around myself and made my way towards Mary's room, yawning as I walked into her room.

"Would think you were the one working most of the night." She smiled at me.

"Shivering count?" I sat on the chair in her room.

"Not unless you be shivering from something a man is doing... no."

"Where did you throw my dress?" I had not seen it when I glanced around the room.

"Tis laying with most of the things I picked up..." she nodded towards a corner of her room, "over there."

"Thank you." I stood up, holding the blanket around myself between an arm and my side as I looked through the various dresses that were laying there until I found it.

"What will you do today?" She turned in her seat, watching me as I turned back around.

"I do not know." I shook my head, dropping the blanket and

pulling my dress over my head in place of it. Remembering the lacing was in the back I shook my head, "I like how the dress you loaned me laced up the front, I need help with this one."

"He bought this from the shop that sells the dresses ready made? Man doing the sewing and sizing?" She guessed as she stood to lace the back up.

"Aye." I nodded.

"Is why we sew our own clothes, makes it easier... not only for us, but for our customers." She giggled.

"I can see why." I waited until she had finished tying me up before turning around, "thank you."

"Do not worry of it. William does not know how to shop for clothing, if he did he would not have bought you a dress that covers your body nor laces up the back." She sat back down.

"He will learn... he seems as if he can be taught."

"He can." She nodded, smiling.

"I am going to head back to where I was staying, collect the cape and find something to do."

"Not find... someone?" She giggled.

"No, he is waiting." I smiled at her.

"Be sure and come back now." She waved, turning back around in her chair and fiddling with items on her dresser.

Making my way out, I dropped the blanket back in the

bedroom and pulled my shoes back on my feet, headed down the staircase and waved at Beth as I left the building. Looking up the clouds were dark, rolling with the wind in them, moving fast and covering every part of the blue sky that tried to show. Wrapping my arms around myself I walked down the street, heading for the entrance to the outer wall that would bring me to the building William had moved me into to begin with. About ten paces from the entrance someone grabbed my arm, spinning around on them I nearly knocked them to their back before I remembered where I was, in public. Looking the man over as he stared at me, he looked familiar, he was medium height, short blonde hair, blue eyes, a thin build. I could not place him in my memory though, even though he looked like someone I had seen before.

"Catherine?" He finally blurted out after staring at me for some time.

"No." I shook my head, trying to turn away as he tightened his grip on my arm. I glared at him, barely turning my head. "Let go of me."

"So...sorry, you just... you look so much like my sister." He let go of my arm.

I walked off, remembering where I recognized him from, this was his sisters body. He had visited with her before she died, took care of the work her mother and father were not seeing to while she lay sick in bed. I thought I had been far enough away from their town that I would not run into anyone who had known her. I quickened my pace, glancing back as he stood there, watching me walk away. Going through the entrance I almost jogged the last pace to the building, opening the door and slamming it behind me. I looked around the room, it lay the same as I had left it. Grabbing the cape I threw it over my shoulders, covering my head with it's hood and pulling it around the front of me to block the cold air. I needed to find William, I needed his horse, it was time to go. As I stepped out of the building, I looked for the boy, he was no where in sight.

    I first made my way to the barracks, looking inside and not finding him. And then to the stables, no one was inside, not even the horses, so stealing one was not an option. I looked behind the stables and barracks where the pen and training area was, having no luck there I turned and left that area. I knew of no where else that he went, given that the horses were gone he was probably riding somewhere. My best bet was to return to the woman's house and lock myself inside somewhere until he returned, and then I would explain why I needed to leave and why I needed a horse.

    Making my way back along the inside of the wall to the entrance, I stopped, looking around it with my mind and not sensing the boy near by. I slid around the side of the entrance so I remained against the wall and made my way down to the woman's house, staying along the wall with the buildings blocking me from view of the street. It was beginning to rain, a freezing cold to it as it fell. As I made it to the end of the row of buildings and the end of the wall, I knew I was at the woman's house. Sliding between the buildings I came out onto the street, people were going inside anywhere they could to get out of the rain. I hurried to the door and went inside where I found numerous men had found themselves in need of a drink and companionship. The boy didn't appear to be inside. Walking back towards the bar with the hood still pulled over my head I found Beth, at her usual spot of filling cups.

    "I need to stay in the room upstairs..." I leaned over, almost whispering to her, "...tell no one but William I am here. I will explain when things slow down."

    "As long as you need." She nodded at me and smiled.

I went to the stairs, took them two at a time going up and let the hood fall once I made it to the top, down the hall and into the room I closed the door behind me. Removing the shoes that were muddy and dropping them near the door I untied the cape and dropped it into the chair before sitting down on the bed. I watched the fireplace, no fire burning inside it any longer, I needed a plan, an escape route.

Chapter Fifty-two

I don't know how long I sat there, but the noise downstairs began to lesson, doors began to close all through the building, the rain began to come down harder. I had blocked out almost everything around me, thinking, planning, waiting. The door burst open and William came inside, drenched head to foot, water dripping from him, he was concerned.

"Mary came to find me. What'is wrong?" He dropped the cape from his shoulders to the floor, not even removing his boots as he normally did upon entering a room.

"I need to leave." I watched him, watching for a reaction of some kind, a change in his energy.

Beth came in, along with Mary, closing the door behind them. Beth offered the explanation, "I sent Mary to find him, you had been up here all day, and the way you came in earlier... I was worried."

"What's wrong girl?" Mary came over, sitting beside me.

"Someone who... someone from another town that knows this body saw me today. I need to leave, without being followed. I need a horse, which is why I need you," I looked at William, then at Beth and Mary, "and until I can leave I need to stay here."

"As long as you need, but..." Beth offered.

"...But what do you mean someone who knows your body?" Mary cut her off.

"This body is not mine. I borrowed it with the permission of the person who had it before me." There was no use trying to come up with a cover for my reasons.

"Wait..." William stepped towards me, "...when you were telling me that... that body was one, and you were another, you literally meant that?"

"I did. The girl who lived in this body, she was dying, the body was sick. I asked her if I could use it to interact with the people here, she gave me her permission. I stayed by her side until she died and then I took the body." I tried to explain it.

"And... you... I do not understand." William shook his head, moving towards the fire to get one going because he was cold, and wet.

"I will show you. Do not start the fire yet." I stood up, walking towards him. I put my hands on his temples, closing my eyes as I transferred the memory of the girl, the body as it died, the way she had seen me and given me permission to use it.

Stepping back he shook his head, "how?"

"When the body is empty, with the permission of the previous owner, the spirit of another may enter it, use it. It is as riding a horse, it is used for transportation, but more than that, it allows the spirit to communicate with others." I tried to put it in the simplest way I could.

"What did you do to him?" Mary looked at me, wanting to know what I had done by putting my hands on his head.

"I transferred my memories, as I saw them, to him. He saw through my eyes." I looked at her, she was not afraid, she was curious. I stepped towards her, "Let me show you... what do you want to see?"

"Show me anything." She stood up so I did not have to reach down to touch her.

"Close your eyes, do not fight me, do not think..." I closed my eyes as I saw hers close. I flooded her mind with images, of the garden where I come from, of Atlantis, of Egypt, of here, of how I saw her and what she looked like through my eyes.

"That is..." She couldn't think of way to explain it as she sat back down, shaking her head.

"And you?" I turned towards Beth.

"I need no images, I can see you are not evil, and I need no proof of who you are. You are, who you are, no one else no matter the outside appearance." She was an accepting woman.

"I need a horse. I need to leave as soon as possible, and I need to go during the night when no one will notice my departure." I turned back to William.

"You can have anything you need, but I am going with you." His eyebrows came together, giving me a stern look as the creases began showing in his forehead, he was thinking. "I need to collect some things, I also need to place someone else in charge so I can leave."

"They will notice if you leave, if I leave no one will notice." I told him. He would be noticed if he went missing, I would not.

"Do not care, I am coming with you." He shook his head, finally removing his boots and sitting down on the edge of the bed. "Beth, can you see to the food and supplies we need? I will provide you with the coins to purchase them."

"Yes, I will do part of it while Mary does the rest." She nodded.

"I will get horse and another animal that can be trusted, you ride with me, will use the other to carry the load. Break for a night, and change the load to horse and will ride the other." He was forming a plan.

"No, you will stay here. I will take a horse, ride a good distance and leave the animal for you to retrieve, continue on foot, leave no trail of the direction I went."

"You are not leaving without me." He tried to assert his authority.

"Watch yourself." I warned him.

"I think we will see to the rest of tonight's duties, you two may work out your plan and inform us of the decision in the morning. Come on Mary." Beth instructed, getting Mary's attention and they left the room.

Chapter Fifty-three

"I am coming." William stood up, towering over me.

"No you are not." I could feel the heat beginning to grow in the palms of my hands, the energy was building with the frustration that was growing.

"Yes, I am."

"I can care of myself. I do not need a man to watch over me."

"I do not care, I am coming with you. That is the end of it. Work out any plan you want, but I am included in it." He moved back towards the fireplace.

"Stop." I told him, I was going to show him something else.

"Why?" He looked back at me.

"I want to show you something, give you an idea of who I am. You need to know before you make your decision." I moved towards the fireplace. I tried not to use the energy to do little things like I was about to do, it wasted energy that could be used towards other needs, fire-stone worked just as well when starting a fire. I closed my eyes, slowly focusing my energy on my hand, allowing it to grow hot, waving my hand over the top of the wood inside the fireplace, flames sparking to life as my hand went over the top.

"What... what did you do?" William stepped towards the fireplace.

"I started the fire." I stood up, watching him, he was confused, but not surprised. "Fire-stone works as easily as anything else, I normally do not waste my energy starting a fire when I can do so with a rock. But it is a sample of what I can do, more of a sample that can be added to what I have shown you already."

"Can you warm me up?" He laughed, finally smiling for the first time this night.

"I can dry your clothes, warm you with my body heat. But no, I am standing by my decision to wait on other methods until I know the cycle." I smiled at him.

"Tis your decision... and I am still going." He smirked.

"Take your clothes off." I laughed at him, he was a stubborn man.

"Why?" He didn't understand my statement.

"The clothes, take them off. I can dry the clothes, but I need them between my hands and I do not wish to burn you." I started grinning, "and the fastest way to warm one with body heat is skin to skin. If you do not wish to catch the fever, I need to warm you as quickly as possible, it even works better than other activities."

"Oh..." He began by pulling his shirt over his head and handing it to me, watching as I closed my hands around part of it, letting the rest hang down. I closed my eyes and focused my heat onto the shirt, drying it from my hands downwards.

"Pants." I set the shirt aside, waiting for him to follow directions. He glanced at me, began to get the red tint to his cheeks as he untied the knot in the lacing at the top band of the pants, untying them and loosening the lacing through the eyelets before pushing them downwards and stepping out of them, handing them to me as well. He was left standing in a white cloth that seemed like short pants. Closing my eyes as I held the pants, I dried them in the same way as I did the shirt.

"You may be more of a use than a fire." He chuckled as I set the pants down on the shirt.

"Are those..." I nodded towards the short pants he was wearing, "wet?"

Glancing down he turned slightly red, "not wet enough that I see need to remove them."

"What are they?"

"Braies." He looked at me as if something had struck him, "under garments. You wear them under your clothes, prevents chaffing and rubbing of the body to a raw point. Items you do not wear."

"Hm..." I stared at them, trying to figure out just how they did what he claimed.

"Is something wrong?" He coughed, drawing my attention back to his face.

"No, just... admiring." I tried not to laugh at the wording I had chosen. "Get into the bed."

"Yes my Lady." He chuckled, following my directions as I

gave them to him.

"Relax, I will not bite... hard." I smiled at him as he crawled under the blanket still on the bed. I picked up the second one and threw it over him. "You may wish to close your eyes."

"Why?"

"Because I do not have any... bra...ees on." It was a strange word, was not easily pronounced. "I am going to remove my dress and instead of turning red, you may wish to close your eyes."

"Will not matter if I see or do not see, I know what you are doing now and will know you are under the blanket without clothing." He closed his eyes anyway, squeezing his lips together and trying to prevent a smirk from crawling onto his face.

Chapter Fifty-four

I had forgotten the dress tied in back, again. I spent some time trying to twist into a position to pull the loop loose, but once it was loose I was able to wiggle the lacing loose, dropping the top of the dress to my hips and pushing it down. Lifting it up as I stepped out of it I laid it on the end of the bed before stepping to the side of the bed. Lifting the blankets and sliding under them, I watched as William squeezed his eyes shut, waiting to be told he could open them.

"Slide over, middle of the bed." I said quietly, "you can open your eyes."

"Hm..." He nodded, moving over to the middle of the bed where I was. He positioned himself flat on his back, his side to me.

"Turn over on your side, face where the window is." I shook my head, trying not to laugh at his respectfulness, it was humorous, but did conflict with the ability to warm him up. "Try to relax." I coached as I slid closer to him, wrapping an arm over his arm and side until my hand was on his chest. My other arm I moved under his head, bending it at the elbow so I could touch his shoulder. My chest was flat against his back, my thighs touching his backside, feet touching his legs as I bent my knees slightly. I closed my eyes and let my body emit the heat from itself, from the inside where the blood coursed through the veins to the skin that touched him. I focused the direction of the heat from my body onto his. I remained chilled as I normally was, one could not warm themselves in this way, it required someone else to do it, but I could emit enough energy and heat from my own body to warm his. As he warmed up, I would begin to warm up.

"You are warm..." He chuckled, keeping his back to me and his hands folded in front of his chest.

"Tis the point of the exercise." I whispered.

"Are you warm... I mean, you feel warm to me, but are you warm?" He didn't know how to ask what he wanted to know.

"No... I cannot warm myself this way. I can only warm you. But as your skin begins to warm, it will warm me." I explained just what I had been thinking.

"Should I... I mean, do you want me to turn over so I can..." he stopped, taking a deep breath and chuckling, "that did not sound the way I mean it. Do you want me to warm you up while you warm me up?"

I sensed the energy from him, he wanted to know if it would work both directions if he held me like I held him, but he did not seem to be able to form the words in the correct order. Smiling, I shook my head, "I am sure we will end up in that position before morning. Tis not a worry right now, I will not get sick but you could."

"Do you get sick?" He tried to look at me by turning his head.

"No..." I shook my head, keeping my eyes closed as I let the heat come off of me.

"How?"

"I am different."

"I know this, but how do you not catch the fever?"

"The body undergoes some changes when it is taken... prevents sickness from setting in."

"Hm..." He turned his head back to look at the curtain over the window. "So you will never get the fever... will you grow old?"

"At a slower rate, but yes, eventually this body will grow old."

"How much slower?" He was curious about everything now.

"When you are an old man, I may look a few, maybe 10 more years than I am now."

He began to move, turning himself over to look at me. Moving his arms around me, I left mine over his side, touching his back now. "Will you grow old?"

"Yes, I will grow old. The body will get creases in it, the skin will sag and stretch out. The body can still die, I cannot stop that." I watched him.

"Why... ho... I want to know so much, but I do not know what to ask." He tried to smile, but it came out more of a snarl. He was curious, and he wanted to understand, but he didn't know what to ask or how to ask it.

"If I was to watch you grow into an old man, I would burn your body years before someone needed to burn mine. I would have to move from town to town, never settling in one place because your people would not understand why I did not age while they died around me." I tried to answer his questions.

"You have watched others die before you?" He was remembering Aree, I had shown him how I had burned her body on the beach.

"Yes... many. I have sent more people to the next life than I care to count. It will always be so, maybe one day it will change, but for now it is as it is. I cannot stop people from dying, I cannot tell the future either."

He nodded, closing his eyes as he tilted his head, adjusting it so that the top of my head rested under his chin, my chest was flat against his and our legs touched. He was thinking, but he didn't want me trying to guess by his facial expressions what he was thinking. I wrapped my arms around him tighter, beginning to absorb the heat from his body, closing my eyes and falling asleep.

Chapter Fifty-five

Waking in the morning, the fire had gone out and the chill had returned to the room. Still in much the same position as the night before the heat from our bodies had kept us warm over night. I thought about the plan, the escape route, I had needed William for a horse but he thought he was going with. I needed to stay here until I could leave, and the women thought they were going to gather supplies. It was going to be a long day, stuck inside of four walls while others planned my plan for me, I almost laughed at the idea.

"Find something funny?" William adjusted so he could look down at me.

"Thought you was sleeping." I tilted my head back so my nose was not against his chest.

"No... awake most of the night."

"Why?"

"Watching the door." Grumbling he laid over onto his back.

"I would sense someone in the room, whether it was friend or foe, I would sense them even in my sleep. You need not lay awake to watch the door." I informed him, something I should have done before we went to sleep, but at least he knew now.

"Hm... could have told me that sooner." He nodded and wiped his hands over his tired face.

"Could have, but did not." I snuggled down into the warmth of the bed, "how do you think I sensed you most times when you entered where I was?"

"I believed you heard me." He looked over at me.

"Sometimes I did, aye... but I knew it was you, without seeing you, because of your energy. I sensed you, felt you enter the room. If it is someone unknown I will sense them that way, if it is someone I know, I will sense who it is." I pulled the blankets over my shoulders.

"You really do not need someone to watch over you?" He turned back over, the creases in his forehead setting in again.

"No, I do not..."

"Does not matter, I am still coming." He flopped back onto his back after breaking in on what I was saying. He did not care what I thought on the subject, he had made his mind up.

"Which direction?" I decided I should know the plan.

"What?" Looking over at me he asked.

"Which direction will we leave in?" I tried to clarify.

"Oh... at night once all the supplies have been gathered, I was thinking out the main road, the meadow, will give us cover in the trees for the night. In the morning we will head for the towns and villages that sit on the sea. Breaking at night to rest the horses and ourselves." He supplied the idea he had.

"I was thinking of traveling at night, less chance someone will see you."

"I cannot see in the dark, neither can my horses..." he looked over at me, "so we travel during the day."

"What do we do when we reach the seas?"

"Take the horses on boat, go to another land across the sea, somewhere that we know people do not know that body." He seriously thought it would work, someplace new, someplace no one knew either of us, would not have to continue moving around because of that but we would have to move because of my lack of aging.

"Okay." I nodded. "I need my dress."

"Wha... oh, yes..." he had forgotten I was naked momentarily. Sitting up he reached across me, grabbing the dress on the edge of the bed and shivering as he gave it to me, sliding back down under the blankets. "You get my clothes once you are dressed, will be fair that you are dressed and can brave the cold first."

Laughing, I pulled the dress under the blankets. Twisting, turning, and wiggling my way back into it before I sat up and walked towards his clothes on the chair, handing them to him before returning to the fireplace. I replaced the logs on it with fresh ones, and again waved my hand over the top setting it into flames.

"How do you do that?" William asked, his clothes still laying on him.

"I imagine flames there, and so there is." I told him how I thought it worked.

"No... I do not mean that." He shook his head, sitting up and pulling his shirt on. "How do you dress and undress under blankets?"

"I move until it is on or off." I laughed.

"Do you not find it difficult not to catch the blanket in your clothes while you do all of that wiggling?"

"No, tis easy... lay back." I walked towards him, grabbing his pants from him, "take these and push them down until you can put your feet inside of them. Than, pull until they are at your knee, brace the blankets up with your knee and wiggle until they are in place."

Shaking his head he gave it a try before finding out that he was not as comfortable with all the wiggling as I was, he stood up and pulled his pants up, tying them off at the top. "I do not care for the movement."

"Your loss, you will dress in the cold from now on then. Tie me up?" I turned my back to him, letting him lace the back of the dress up.

"Will need a few more of these, change of shoes, and a warmer cape for you to put over your other one." I listened as he finished tying the loop into the neck of the dress.

"And you will need?" I turned around.

"I have all of that for myself, but you will need it. I also have travel gear, is for when we are at battle but will work for this as well." He nodded, heading for his boots by the door. "Will leave a list of dry foods and vegetables for Beth and Mary to get for us today. I will remain gone until night fall, bring the horses round the back and leave them while I collect the items and you. We can leave tonight."

"I will be here, no where else." I laughed, feeling the walls begin to move in when I realized I would be inside all day, right where I was.

"Will see to my duties and set someone I trust in charge, break away and collect some items before I return. All will be done today." He reassured himself as much as anyone.

"Then see to them before we have a man on our door." I smiled at him, reminding him of the man who insisted on either coming in or knocking on the door the past few mornings.

"Stay put." He looked at me, not fully trusting that I was going to wait for him as he pulled the door open, "I will be back." He closed the door behind him as he left the room, his cape thrown over his arm.

Sitting in this room was going to require a guard at the door... T'would not be easy watching the walls and the fire place. Again I would have nothing to do and too much time to worry over the fact that there was nothing to do.

Chapter Fifty-six

The sun was peaking through the curtain hanging over the window, creating colored light on the floor of the room. The fireplace was black from the fires that had burned in it, soot covering the sides of it. A sense of upheaval washed over the room, the entire building, I heard chairs scrape the floor on the level below as the sound of footsteps hurried out of the doors that slammed behind whoever left. Someone was here, someone without good intentions. Getting up off the edge of the bed where I sat cross legged watching the room, I made my way barefooted towards the door, opening it slightly and listening to the voices downstairs.

"...know she is here." A male voice was speaking, I didn't recognize it.

"You need to leave." Informing whoever it was Beth had a threatening tone to her voice.

"We have seen Sir William with her, he has been spending his time here as of late. Where is she?" The voice persisted.

"I said leave." I heard Beth tell them again, a firmer sense about her voice.

Closing my eyes I looked at what was happening. There were three of the knights downstairs, a man in a long black dress holding a book with a gold colored object hanging around his neck, and there was the boy who had stopped me the day before.

"Beth, put the log down." One of the Knights stepped towards Beth who was holding the log she had told me about. Mary was standing at the base of the steps, a few of the other girls peeked out of their rooms or stood on the stairs.

"She has been charged with sorcery, tis for the benefit of all that she is executed." The man in the black dress spoke a strange language, "God does not want any of his children tainted by her spells."

"She is not a witch, and she is not here!" Beth glared at the man.

"No, she is not a witch, but a demon. Took this boy's poor sister, made her sick and killed her to take the body so she could do the work of the devil with God's children." The man was slowly moving towards Beth.

"Beth, just tell us where she is, we will leave once she is in our hold." The Knight who had done all the talking tried to talk to Beth as if she needed to understand. "She has Sir William under a spell, the only way he will be released is if she is dead. The only way you, and your girls, will be safe and forgiven is if she is no longer here."

Movement caught my attention near the stairs, one of the Knights had moved towards Mary who blocked his way. He was trying to move her out of the way when she took a swing at him, if it had been under any other circumstances I may have found it funny, she did not seem like the kind of person to strike anyone.

"Move wench!" The Knight pushed her aside, forcing his way up the stairs.

I could feel the protective feeling building inside of me, no one handled my friends that way. As a jolt of what felt like electricity hit me I opened my eyes, back in my body near the door. Pulling it the rest of the way open I stepped out of it, heading for the top of the stairs as the girls peering out of their rooms closed the doors to them. As my foot touched the top step of the stairs, the Knight who had pushed Mary was halfway up them, stopping where he was and watching me as if I was going to breathe fire at him. I smiled, placing my hand on the railing and hoping over the side of it. Dropping down to the bottom floor, almost kneeling as my feet hit the wood of the floor. I looked at the man in the dress, he was cleaner than most people here, he must have washed daily. He wore a leather belt around his stomach, a pouch hanging from it. The boy, Catherine's brother, watched me, almost afraid to move as if my sight depended on movement.

"Do not take another step." The man in the dress glared at me. He seemed as if he commanded some kind of power and obedience of most people, but what he did not understand was that I answered to no one. I stepped towards him, intending on backing him down, the Knights kept their distance from me and the boy did not move, if this man could be backed down, the others would leave. "I command you to stop!" He held his book in front of his chest.

"What is that?" I nodded towards the book, drawing his attention from me to the book.

"Tis the Holy Words of God, the Bible." He seemed almost offended that I didn't know what it was.

"And that around your neck?" I put his attention onto the golden item he wore.

"The Cross that our Savior, the Son of God, died on for our

sins." He backed up.

"And you?" I stepped towards him again, he was beginning to doubt his power.

"I am a messenger of God, I... I am his servant, I commune between him and his children here on Earth." He backed up again.

"Have you met him?" I took another step towards him, watching him begin to tremble where he was.

"God is with us always."

"Is he now? And who is your God?" I tilted my head, watching every breath he took.

"He... he is..." the man swallowed hard, hugging the book tighter to his chest as he backed into a chair, "Our Father, Who Aught in Heaven, Reins over the Kingdom of Earth."

I started smiling, I knew exactly who he was talking about, and his image of the man was going to be shattered into a thousand little pieces by the time I was done with him. "Your God, is an evil man." I shook my head at him, never taking my eyes from him. "He kills by the thousands, he saves only those he wants for breeding, he cares nothing for you and your kind. I met him once..." I nodded as I stepped closer to the little round man, "he surrounds himself by others of his kind, as if he is afraid to face anyone on his own. Almost took his life as well, but I failed that time. He snarls like a animal foaming at the mouth, destroying everything he touches..."

"Enough demon!" The man held his little golden cross out in front of him with his free hand.

"You think that is going to protect you?" I took another step towards him.

"By the power of God, I command you to stop." His hand shook slightly. He was beginning to become afraid.

"Make me..." I snarled at him, almost enjoying the way he doubted himself, his God. No, he wouldn't admit it, but I could feel it radiating off of him like a bad smell. Taking the last few steps between him and myself, I reached my hands out and grabbed his head, forcing the images of Draconus into his mind. The snarl he possessed as he set foot on Atlantis, the blood that turned the waters and sand red, the bodies of everyone covering the ground. I showed him exactly who his God was, I showed him who he was worshiping, who he thought was going to protect him.

"Exorcizo te, omnis spiritus immunde, in nomine Dei..." the man began speaking through the images I was giving him, "...Patris omnipotentis, et in noimine Jesu Christi Filli ejus, Domini et Judicis nostri, et in virtute Spiritus Sancti, ut descedas ab hoc plasmate Dei Catherine, quod Dominus noster ad templum sanctum summ vocare dignatus est, ut fiat templum Dei vivi, et Spiritus Sanctus habitet in eo. Per eumdem Christum Dominum nostrum, qui venturus est judicare vivos et mortuos, et saeculum per ignem." As his speech came to an end, I felt liquid thrown on my face.

"What?" I wiped my face of the liquid that was thrown onto it. "What was that?"

"H...Ho...Holy Water." He leaned back as far onto the table as his body would let him without laying on it.

"You threw water on me? And what's that going to do, give me a bath?" I shook my head, rolling my eyes at him as he dipped the small bottle he held on his fingers again, as he lifted them, intending to throw another round on me, I grabbed his throat. "Do not." I shook my head, warning him I was in no need of a bath.

"Exorcizo te, omnis spiritus immunde, in nomine Dei Patris omnipotentis..." He began trying to speak again as I tightened my grip on his throat, choking the words out of his body along with the air.

"Silence." I glared at him. "I am not a demon, or a witch, or here to kill anyone... unless Draco and his pack want to come and play. If I let go of you, are you going to remain quiet?" I waited until the man in the dress nodded before I let go of his throat.

Chapter Fifty-seven

"Arrest her!" He yelped as soon as I let go of his throat, he began rubbing his throat and sliding away from the table.

"In the name of the King you are hereby arrested and charged with sorcery." One of the Knights grabbed my right arm as he spoke, another grabbed my left arm not long after the first finished speaking.

"Sorry Beth." I looked at Beth, all of her business had been chased out of the building by the little round man in the dress.

"Tis okay..." she responded, Mary standing next to her.

"Take her outside." The little man ordered.

I was marched out the door like a prisoner by the Knights in their armor, the boy followed behind them, and the annoying man behind him. I sensed Beth and Mary behind him, not but a few steps behind him. The people who had been chased from the building were standing outside in the street that was covered in thick, wet mud from the rain the night before. More were gathering around the further down the street we went. People came out of their homes, the buildings, hugging children to them and watching.

"Here will be fine." The round little man spoke, bringing the Knights to a stop. They tightened their grip on my arms waiting to be instructed as to what to do next. "This woman has been possessed by a demon who first made her sick, and then saw to it that she died so that it could take her body. The devil has sent his minions to taint this town through witchcraft and sorcery." The man looked around at everyone gathering nearby. "Be this a lesson to always pray to our Father for the safety of our children and blessings to our King for he and his family are the chosen rulers by birth. I have found that the demon cannot be exorcised from the body of this poor woman, because of this I have determined that the woman's soul is being held captive inside and will not be allowed to go to Heaven and join our Father or his son, Jesus Christ. By order of the most high, I sentence this demon to die by beheading, may it return to Satan and the soul of the woman be forgiven for the sins that have been committed."

There was a commotion around, gasps and fearful screams as many of the people made the sign of the cross over their chests and over their children, people began reciting different things, I assumed it was something close to what the round little man had said. Jesus Christ's, Holy Father's, Virgin Mary's and all kinds of other non-sense flowed from their mouths.

Looking at the annoying man in the dress, I decided to tell him the truth. "You are correct in your assumption I am not Catherine. She was sick and dying when I found her, I stayed with her until she died. She gave me permission to use her body. I promise, I am not here to harm anyone."

"Silence demon!" He felt in control now that I was restrained from choking the life out of his body.

"I am not Catherine, but I did have her permission. I asked!" I was growing tired of his mindless comments.

"On your knees... Pray to the Lord to save your soul. I cannot give forgiveness for the wickedness you have committed."

"There is no way, on any planet, that I would bow down to that scaly piece of scum!" I glared at the man.

The knights that held my arms pulled back with one hand while they pushed on my back with their other hand, creating a pain between my shoulder blades that forced me to drop to my knees. Once down, they continued to hold my back down and my arms upwards behind me.

"You are hereby charged with sorcery, demonic possession of Catherine Joans." The book holding, water throwing little man standing in front of me was spouting off a whole reterhic of nonsense once again, I couldn't help but roll my eyes at him, even his voice was scratchy. "By the grace of God I order your immediate death, may you burn in the fires of damnation for all time." Making the sign of the cross over my head he stepped back.

"I am not Catherine, I had her permission!" I decided to make my plea once more to keep the body which only caused the Knights to tighten their grip on my arms which they were holding behind my back.

"What is..." I heard William's voice in the crowed, looking up he was forcing his way through the people gathered.

"William..." I began, watching him come to a complete halt as he looked down at me on my knees. His face had shock written all over it before he forced his mouth closed and forced it not to show.

"May God take pity upon this young woman's soul." The round man was again scratching at the ears of any present as he held his book tighter to his chest. He raised his arm as the third Knight stepped around to my side, dropping his arm he signaled the Knight to kill me. Looking up for a moment, I looked at

William who closed his eyes, slumping in his posture as the Knight dropped his sword.

For a brief moment, I felt the blade connect with the skin of the back of my neck, slicing downwards, I felt blood momentarily as it cut through the skin, the pressure was on the backbone that ran through the neck, severing the head from the body.

Everything went black once again, not a sound around me, no feeling, no senses. As I felt the cold begin to set it, I opened my eyes in time to watch the force shield collapse in front of me, dropping me from stasis as the liquid from inside poured onto the floor along with my body.

"That was a short trip." The technician standing over me felt the need to comment on my abrupt return.

"Put me back in." I looked up at him.

"Body needs to readjust before I can put you back in, you know that." He turned away from me, waving two others over, "get her on the table."

As they lifted the body up I felt the tingling begin to set it, causing pains throughout my body wherever it moved. "I need to go back."

"I am not putting you back in right now, go with your mind." He told me I was stuck as he pulled the machine over my body, scanning for any problems from coming out of stasis.

Closing my eyes, I shut out my home, the people around me and forced my mind to leave the body it had been shot back into. I focused myself on Beth, on Mary, on William, willing myself back to them. Every sound died out around me, all light around me blacked out, and the next thing I knew I was standing in the woman's building, in the room I had been staying in. William was sitting on the bed, holding the dress Mary had let me wear. Mary was laying on the bed crying. Beth was pouring liqueur from a jug into cups, dry tears on her cheeks.

Moving forwards I rested my hand on Beth's shoulder, sending my energy into her and giving her an image of the buildings at home, as her head came up, she looked around the room and smiled.

I moved towards Mary next, laying down on the bed next to her and resting my hand on her head, giving her images of the garden outside the castle, of the water that ran, she stopped crying and closed her eyes, breathing slowly.

Moving from the bed, I walked until I was in front of William, standing there I watched him for a moment. He had tears building in his eyes but he refused to cry, shaking my head I smiled, he was a stubborn man. I rested both of my hands on his shoulders, passing on images of him laughing, smiling as I had seen him do.

I sent feelings of happiness to him as I began to give him my thoughts, I spoke to him in his mind. *"Thank you for showing me that all is not lost in this world. I will come back, maybe in this life, maybe in another, but I will come back."*

He looked up from the dress, almost as if he was looking right at me, and then he let his grief go, releasing all of the pent up negativity he was feeling. I felt his energy change as Beth and Mary's had, he no longer felt guilt, nor did he feel hatred for the other Knights or the brother, or the cross wearing man. He smirked, shaking his head, as he whispered his response to my thoughts "I will wait."

Flooding the room with energy as the light came through the window, I gave them all a warm feeling, surrounding them in happiness and love. I left part of me there as I backed out of the room, watching as they breathed me in and knew everything would be okay. Smiling to myself I turned from the room with the images of them forever embedded on my spirit.

Returning home, I opened my eyes to find the Prince standing over me. He smiled down at me, "a little too quick... I was beginning to enjoy my break of you."

"Tis nice to see you as well." I glared at him, "now get out of my face."

He laughed, leaving the room I had been placed in, "glad to have you back."

I laid there, thinking of the short trip, how I had despised what Earth had become only to find that not everything had changed. There were still people there that deserved to be free, it was a reminder of what I trained for every day of my life.

I would return, and I would find them again.